AT HOME IN THE HEARTLAND

ROBERT WINTER | ALEXANDER VERTIKOFF

AT HOME IN THE HEARTLAND

MIDWESTERN DOMESTIC ARCHITECTURE

Gibbs Smith, Publisher
TO ENRICH AND INSPIRE HUMANKIND
Salt Lake City | Charleston | Santa Fe | Santa Barbara

First Edition
11 10 09 08 07 5 4 3 2 1

Published by
Gibbs Smith, Publisher
P.O. Box 667
Layton, Utah 84041

1.800.835.4993 orders
www.gibbs-smith.com

Designed and produced by Kurt Hauser
Printed and bound in China

Library of Congress Cataloging-in-Publication Data

Winter, Robert, 1924–
At home in the heartland : midwestern domestic architecture /
Robert Winter, Alexander Vertikoff.—1st ed.
p. cm.
Includes bibliographical references and index.
ISBN-13: 978-1-58685-799-8
ISBN-10: 1-58685-799-1
1. Architecture, Domestic—Middle West.
I. Vertikoff, Alexander. II. Title.

NA7218.W56 2007
728.0977-dc22 2006028147

Dard Hunter House
"Mountain House":
the stained-glass window

Dedicated to Nora,
who is married to Alex,
and who reads Bob's text.

CONTENTS

viii Preface: *At Home in the Heartland: How This Book Came About*

xi Introduction

1 ONE · **LOG HOUSE**

French Interpretation

Le Poincet House 1

Yankee Log Cabin

Dunn Cabin 5

Galloway Cabin 6

Lincoln Cabins 8

Sargeant Farm 10

13 TWO · **GEORGIAN MODE**

Boone Cabin 12

Worthington Building 15

17 THREE · **CLASSICAL REVIVAL**

Small Town: Madison, Indiana

Sullivan House 18

Lanier Mansion 22

Shrewsbury House 24

Costigan House 26

Elsewhere

Avery House 29

33 FOUR · **AGE OF CHANGE**

Gothic Revival

Hunter House, "Mountain House" 36

"American Gothic" House 41

Neff Cottage 42

Owen Laboratory 43

Gothic Revival House 44

Italianate

Gaff Mansion, "Hillforest" 45

Pratt House, "Honolulu House" 50

Octagon House 52

French Second Empire (Mansard)

Iowa Governor's Mansion, "Terrace Hill" 53

Missouri Governor's Mansion 58

Queen Anne
Hackley House 65
Richardsonian
Proudfoot House, "Hillside Cottage" 72
Studebaker House 76

79 FIVE · **AGE OF REFORM**
Shingle Style
Freer House 78
Beaux-Arts
Conn House 84
Morton House, "Arbor Lodge" 88
Prairie Style
Tomek House 90
Franke House 94
Foursquare House 100
Tudor Revival
White House, "Red Rocks" 101
Evans House 103
Chicago Bungalow
Thomas Bungalow 109

115 SIX · **MODERNISM**
Century-of-Progress Exposition, 1933–1934 116
Usonian
Christian House, "Samara" 118
Rush Creek Village 122
Smith Farm 124
Expressionism
Ford House 128
International Style
Farnsworth House 134
Morrow House 141
Lustron House 144
Modern Vernacular
Harris House 149

154 Bibliographical Note
155 Index
160 Acknowledgments

AT HOME IN **THE HEARTLAND:**

HOW THIS BOOK CAME ABOUT

In the fall of 2003, architectural historian Pamela Kingsbury and I led a tour of the Midwest for the Society of Architectural Historians. We called it the "Heartland Tour." Since we had only a week in which to show the sights, we chose a route from Des Moines to Wichita, believing it contained enough of the Midwest for our fellow travelers to get a taste of a culture that is only dimly perceived by most architectural historians. In Des Moines, we visited the Art Center, whose original building is by Eliel Saarinen, with later additions by I. M. Pei and Richard Meier, and then visited buildings by Mies van der Rohe and Eero Saarinen at Drake University. On our way to Sioux City with its amazing Woodbury County Courthouse by George Grant Elmslie, we spent a good deal of time (some thought too much) at Ida Grove, Iowa, where Byron Godberson, a local manufacturer of machinery, was so taken with Gothic architecture that he paid for its use on a number of buildings, including a McDonald's. After having a reception in Elmslie's courthouse, we went on to Omaha where we saw its wonderful Joslyn Art Museum, a mixture of Beaux-Arts and Art Deco forms, and then to Lincoln to explore Bertram Goodhue's Nebraska State Capitol. We ended our tour at Frank Lloyd Wright's Prairie-style Allen House in Wichita.

It was an exhausting trip—we covered over a thousand miles—but we sold many in the group on the significance of the architecture of the Midwest, in addition to a recognition of its beautiful undulating prairie. Why not, I thought, expand this experience into a book on the variety of Midwestern architecture.

My friend and co author, Alex Vertikoff, and I decided to take on the whole of the Midwest—well, not quite the whole, for we left out the western two-thirds of Kansas and Nebraska and all of the Dakotas on the grounds that these areas had less notable domestic architecture than other parts of the Midwest. Likewise, we omitted Wisconsin and Minnesota because they had too much.

I located the potential candidates for inclusion from experience or from books in my library. One useful resource was *The Guide to Early American Homes, North and South* that Dorothy and Richard Pratt published in 1956. The Pratts had keen eyes and great curiosity, which led them to many a significant building. A half century later, many of the beautifully restored and furnished houses that they chose have been converted to bed-and-breakfasts, restaurants, and house museums, and are thus open to the public. The well-written WPA guides of the late thirties usually had at least one architecture buff on their staffs who called attention to the best buildings in the many towns and cities of America. And by now, the art of writing architectural guidebooks has advanced even into small towns. The resources are there.

About forty buildings have emerged from books, tips from friends, and our own travels. Obviously we highlight what we think are some of the best houses of all periods. We have missed many museum houses, sometimes because their owners or directors imposed fees for photography. We do not mind paying for the reproduction of images, but we do think it unnecessary to charge stiff fees for the taking of photographs that will only increase the number of visitors coming to their buildings.

Most historical societies and preservation organizations who supervise museum houses have not even mentioned fees. All but one owner of highly recommended private houses answered my plea for permission to enter and photograph the premises. In fact, most of them were delighted that we thought so much of their homes. We have made many new friends.

Alex and I were both raised in the Midwest, he in Columbus, Ohio, and I in Elkhart, Indiana. We hope that this book will be looked upon as a tribute to the architects of the Midwest and to their clients who made the realization of their ideas possible, and to the present owners of significant houses who have restored and maintained them with intelligence and love.

INTRODUCTION

If epic poetry were still in fashion, the westward movement in nineteenth-century America would provide rich material. The filling up of the area between the Atlantic and the Pacific and the joys and griefs thereof compose the history that brings all Americans together. And it is the Middle West, or in its shorthand version, the Midwest, that is at the center of this story because, even today when its farms have been urbanized, it embodies the pastoral image that we like to live with. It is still the Heartland.

The Midwest is made up of lands that at one time or another were ruled by Great Britain, France, and Spain, and even earlier were occupied by American Indians. The boundaries of the Midwest are roughly the Rocky Mountains on the west, the Canadian border on the north, the Appalachian Mountains on the east and the southern state boundaries of Kansas and Missouri and the Ohio River on the south. This would include the old Northwest Territory ceded by the former British colonies to the federal government after the American Revolution and opened for settlement by the Northwest Ordinance of 1787. In 1803, the Louisiana Purchase greatly extended this territory.

Geographically it consists of a prairie once covered with grasslands extending from what is now eastern Indiana to the lower Rockies. Forests existed in Ohio, southern Indiana, and the Great Lakes region, but the prairie was almost treeless except for vegetation along its many creeks and rivers. At the same time it was (and is) extremely fertile land, easy to farm except in its western limits where droughts frequently occur. The summers, particularly along the Ohio River, are hot and humid and the winters cold, but normally Midwestern farmers can produce good crops, and the productivity of their land has become a testimony to the special grace that God gave to the American people.

Nevertheless, the settlement of the Midwest was arduous. Nature had to be conquered before farming could begin. The Appalachian Mountains were easily scaled and the semi-nomadic Indians were pushed ever westward. As the Yankee migrants advanced beyond the mountains, they ran into forests; trees standing in the way of farms became the enemy. But the greatest problems lay farther on in the vast distances that had to be traversed and the difficulties of communication and transportation that had to be resolved. Fortunately for the would-be settlers, the means were at hand to remedy these difficulties.

First of all, the navigable rivers were natural channels for migration and trade. The Ohio River, originating in Pennsylvania, served migrants from the Middle Atlantic states and, flowing south then west, accommodated people from the southeastern states. It emptied into the Mississippi, which was another artery that directed settlers to the northern Midwest—so was the Missouri River, branching off on a diagonal through Missouri, Kansas, Nebraska, and the Dakotas, further distributing the population.

The Great Lakes aided immigration and the flow of farm products and minerals to eastern markets. But just as important were the canals that, after the opening of the Erie Canal in 1825, were popular public works. They remained so until the railroads made them outmoded in the 1840s. The most significant of these canals for the development of the Midwest was the Wabash and Erie Canal (1835–1853) that connected the Maumee River in Ohio with the Wabash River in Indiana and, with further improvements, made it possible to navigate boats between Toledo, Ohio, on Lake Erie to Evansville, Indiana, on the Ohio River in the southwestern corner of the state. The Wabash and Erie Canal covered 468 miles and was the largest man-made waterway in the Western Hemisphere at the time.

At least in the eastern Midwest the canal boat took precedence over the prairie schooner. The latter needed roads and sometimes these were exceedingly primitive. The better ones were built using logs as a roadbed. These were called corduroy roads and were at the mercy of nature and hard use. A great improvement came with the use of macadam (layers of crushed rock), an English invention. The National Road (the present Route 40) was authorized by Congress in 1806 and was completed between Cumberland, Maryland, and Vandalia, Illinois, in the 1840s. At first, it was paved with corduroy or loose gravel, but by the 1840s, macadam became the building material most used.

What really brought the Midwest (and the country) together was the system of railroads that by the time of the Civil War crisscrossed the land in a network that was the economic bulwark of the heartland. The trunk lines going mostly east and west—the Burlington Route, New York Central, the Baltimore and Ohio—are still remembered even in the age of Amtrak. But it is hard to imagine the complex pattern of networks of short lines that once serviced the farmers as well as the industrialists in the Midwest, especially since today most of the tracks are gone. But in the nineteenth century, every town insisted on a railroad connection, even if it had to pay for it.

Examples of today's architectural boom in the Midwest.

So far, we have traced the Yankee invasion of the Midwest. It also lured the European emigrant. The Napoleonic wars of the late eighteenth and early nineteenth centuries had stirred up European politics. Nationalism fostered unification movements accompanied by warfare and intolerance between ethnic groups. Naturally, such unrest caused consternation among people who wanted to achieve their independence and to protect their culture. America, and especially the Midwest, was a haven for the discontented. On the lonely prairie, they could preserve their old institutions. The Europeans came, and they brought their cultures with them.

Germans came not only to eastern havens such as Brooklyn in New York but also to towns and farms along the Mississippi. Sephardic Jews founded Reformed Judaism in Cincinnati. All the Irish did not settle in Boston. They became police officers and politicians in Chicago and elsewhere. The Scandinavians found Minnesota a good place to live and advance their social systems. The Poles loved Chicago. And, as everyone knows, the great Czech composer Antonín Dvorák found a bit of his homeland in Spillville, Iowa, and played the pipe organ there in a little church that still exists. (Incidentally, he found the prairie "sad unto despair.") Every European culture was represented in the Midwest in the nineteenth century.

This book is an essay on the unity of American culture. Essentially, the architecture of the Midwest echoes that of the rest of the country. We have organized this book on a rundown of the styles. This move is partly didactic, but it also allows us to show variations within the styles. For example, the beautiful house called "Hillforest," in Aurora, Indiana, clearly falls into the Italian Villa–style category, but it is otherwise unlike any other Italian Villa in the United States. It is almost the exact opposite of A. J. Davis' picturesque Italianate "Litchfield" with its irregular floor plan and picturesque tower. Designed by Isaiah Rogers, one of the finest American architects of the time, Hillforest reflects the quality of his imagination.

The house crowns a hill and has a great view of the Ohio River far below it. It is unique on its site. This fact suggests that, even though the styles may be the same all over North America, their introduction into a variety of landscapes changes our perception of them. Mies's Farnsworth house clearly contrasts with its beautiful but informal natural setting and would be seen quite differently on a city grid. A bald nondescript farmhouse placed in the rolling green hills of southern Iowa belies its Spartan simplicity and evokes a Grant Wood painting. On flatter land, it might seem lonely and sad. These changing perspectives enhance the depth of our experience.

There is much more to say about the Midwest, and much will be said in the pages that follow. It represents symbolically the America that was lost when the machine age advanced. We cling to the pastoral image when its reality is almost gone—but not forgotten.

AT HOME IN **THE HEARTLAND**

ONE

LOG HOUSE

FRENCH INTERPRETATION

Historians of the United States have usually begun their texts with subjects on the East Coast. Then they add a short reference to French settlement west of the Appalachians when discussing the French and Indian War (1755–1763). The French come up again when Thomas Jefferson's purchase of the Louisiana Territory from the French in 1803 is noted. The truth is that the French had a long history of involvement in America, beginning their exploitation of the land east of the Mississippi as early as the seventeenth century. Their aim was not necessarily to colonize the area but to collect its beaver skins. Nevertheless, towns did develop around trading posts.

Cahokia, founded in 1699, is one of these. Along with several other French towns on the Mississippi above New Orleans, it became an outpost of French influence. The town was actually founded by missionaries who were intent on Christianizing the large number of American Indians who already lived in the area. The holy men were followed by settlers who traveled the waterways from Canada in order to work the fertile soil and participate in the fur trade. By the early eighteenth century, there was a chance that Cahokia might become a major commercial center, but hopes were dashed by the growth of Spanish St. Louis, almost directly across the Mississippi River.

Le Poincet House · restored, 1939 · *Cahokia, Illinois*

Le Poincet House (c. 1740), later called the Saucier House, was a product of the period of the greatest French success. It was built by a method commonly used in the domestic architecture of Normandy, from which many of the immigrants came. John Reynolds, an Englishman who lived in Cahokia in the 1780s, described the houses that he studied. They were, he said, "generally one story high and made of wood."

Le Poincet House

> These houses were formed of large posts or timbers; the posts being three or four feet apart in many of them. In others the posts were closer together, and the intervals filled up with mortar, made of common clay and cut straw. . . . Over the whole wall, outside and inside it was generally white-washed with fine white lime, so that these houses presented a clean, neat appearance. . . . Some dwelling houses and the stables and barns were made of longer posts set in the ground, instead of a sill as used in other houses. These posts were of cedar and other durable wood. . . . The covering of the houses, stables, etc., was generally of straw or long grass cut in the prairie. These thatched roofs looked well, and lasted longer than shingles. They were made steep and neat. All the houses, almost, had galleries all around them. The posts of the gallery were generally of cedar or mulberry. The floors of the galleries, as well as the floors of the houses, were made of puncheons [a heavy broad piece of roughly dressed timber with one side hewed flat], as sawed boards were scarce.

Le Poincet House fits the description of the post-on-sill (*poteaux-sur-solle*) structure. In order to expose the construction, the whitewash has been omitted in the present very-much-reconstructed house.

In fact, the history of the rebuildings of this house offers many lessons to preservationists and to modern observers who expect to encounter some semblance of authenticity when they look at an old building. During the nineteenth century, Le Poincet house functioned at various times as a home, a warehouse, a courthouse, and then late in the century as the notorious "Old Courthouse Saloon," where bibulous crowds held mock trials and, as one observer noted, "laughter and rowdiness replaced the law."

Frequent floods of the Mississippi River rotted many of the logs. Finally, an East St. Louis businessman bought what was left of the house and stored the logs in his backyard. When the Louisiana Purchase Exposition opened in 1904, the building was hauled across the river and reconstructed on the fairgrounds in St. Louis, but about two feet were sawed off the rotted bases of the logs, and what was left was put together without chinking. The result was that the house was about a third of its original size. The roofline was altered and, according to contemporary accounts, the leftover wood was made into imitation cigars that were given away as souvenirs.

After the fair, the remains of the house were removed to Chicago, and after another reconstruction, the building became a Japanese tearoom. You might suppose that the people of Cahokia would have forgotten it by then, but a few resident history buffs began a campaign for its return to the city; finally, in 1939, it was brought back and restored by the New Deal Works Progress Administration (WPA).

Luckily, old photographs existed of the house as it stood in the late nineteenth century, and these served as the basis for reconstruction on its old foundations. But many new logs had to be used so that about two-thirds of the house is relatively new work. As it stands today, it is a well-intentioned and reasonably educated fabrication of history.

LE POINCET HOUSE

YANKEE LOG CABIN

It is now common knowledge that the log cabin house type, so important in the settlement of America from the eastern seaboard to the Rockies, was an import. It was not invented by the Indians, as was originally supposed, but was developed in northern Europe in the seventeenth century and perhaps earlier. In fact, many eighteenth-century palaces and churches in Russia were constructed of logs laid horizontally and then faced with stucco or stone.

It was probably the Swedes, whose colony was on the Delaware River, who introduced the northern European log cabin to America in the seventeenth century. Then in the late eighteenth century, the idea was spread along the rivers, lakes, canals, and roads into the interior of America, where it was employed in settlements throughout the West. In fact, the greatest numbers of log cabins today, often covered with shingles or clapboards, are found along the old National Road that eventually stretched across the Midwest from the Ohio River at Wheeling, West Virginia; through Columbus, Ohio, and Indianapolis, Indiana; and on to Vandalia, Illinois.

Usually, log cabins were intended to be temporary structures. But for many years in the nineteenth century, especially in the age of Andrew Jackson, they became symbols of democracy and the simple life. It was thought to be politically advantageous to have been born in one. Abraham Lincoln scored well in this category. When William Henry Harrison, who was born in a Virginia mansion, ran for the presidency in 1840, the Republican Party adopted the log cabin as its symbol. Franklin Roosevelt's Secretary of State, Cordell Hull, supposedly was the last politician to have been born in a log cabin. But there may be more.

Joseph Smith Cabin, "The Homestead" • 1823 • Nauvoo, Illinois
north addition (right) by Joseph Smith Jr., 1840
west addition (far left) by Joseph Smith III, 1858

There is no doubt that the log cabin is picturesque. Constructed of notched (rarely mortised) logs, it is the ultimate Arts and Crafts house and thus has a certain contemporary resonance. It may be significant that in Japan today there is a magazine called *Woody*, completely devoted to that nation's interest in the quaint log cabin.

(Author's Note: I am deeply indebted to Donald A. Hutslar's book *The Log Architecture of Ohio* [1977] for information in this short essay.)

Dunn Cabin • c. 1795 • *Cincinnati, Ohio* ▹

Galloway Cabin · c. 1797 · *Zenia, Ohio*

Galloway Cabin:
the upstairs guestroom,
with stairs leading to
a bedroom in the attic,
the front entrance,
the basement fireplace,
which was originally
used as a kitchen

GALLOWAY CABIN

LINCOLN CABIN:
the kitchen hearth,
the front entries,
the smokehouse

Abraham Lincoln Cabin

· 1835–37; rebuilt, 1935 ·

Reconstruction on foundations of original house near Lerna, Illinois

LINCOLN CABIN

Sargeant Farm · c. 1836–43 · *Historic cabin near Lerna, Illinois*

SARGEANT FARM

TWO

GEORGIAN MODE

Georgian architecture is rare in the Midwest. After all, it was disappearing as a popular building style by the time the Old Northwest was opened for settlement. A little can be found in Ohio, less in Indiana and Illinois. It is therefore unusual to find any at all by the time the settlers reached the Mississippi River.

 NATHAN BOONE HOUSE · c. 1810 · *Defiance, Missouri*

The Nathan Boone House, ensconced near the bank of the Missouri River at its confluence with the Mississippi, is a real rarity. The reader should be warned that, although the house is arranged in the Georgian manner—bilateral symmetry, central hall, and staircase with rooms at each side—the strong Georgian effect comes from the addition of the simple classical pediment over the front door and the shutters, none of which are original to the house but put there quite recently to make the house look more presentable.

There are other imaginative touches, some of them in interpretation. For example, there is no doubt that the first tenant of the house was the son of Daniel Boone, the symbol of the independent frontiersman, a pragmatist careless of precedent, and, above all, self-reliant. There is no doubt that Daniel Boone died in this house, but there is also a story that he spent the last years of his life carving the elaborate classically ornamented mantelpieces for it. The sophistication of their design would seem to contradict the notion presented by famous American historian Frederick Jackson Turner that the settlers of the Midwest threw off European institutions as they moved west and then created new ones. The existence of these mantelpieces and the fact that they were installed sometime in the early nineteenth century certainly casts doubt on the validity of Turner's hypothesis. Nevertheless, according to Boone's biographer, John Mack Faragher, there is not a shred of evidence that Boone had anything to do with their carving. Boone's craftsmanship may be in doubt, but even without the granny-tale, the existence of these

 BOONE HOUSE

Boone House: the drawing room, the mantelpiece

beautifully designed mantelpieces, possibly crafted in nearby St. Louis or imported from the East, does suggest that the frontiersmen were not iconoclasts.

The galleried porch to the rear of the house was a fairly recent addition. Very little of the furniture inside the house is original, though it is of the period and certainly looks good. Nevertheless, its use should make us leery of our ability to see historic architecture exactly as the original owners saw it. But the siting of the house on a rise toward a hillside covered with woods and its view down through pastures to the Missouri River give it an authenticity of place that allows us to imagine that we are on the frontier even when civilization is nearby.

Worthington Building · 1806–7 · *Chillicothe, Ohio* ▹

THREE

CLASSICAL REVIVAL

As we have seen, the oldest European settlements in what we now call the Midwest were in the Mississippi and Missouri river valleys—and they were French, not Yankee. In the East, settlement west of the Appalachians was all but prevented until after the American Revolution and the passage of the Ordinance of 1787, which made possible a relatively orderly occupation of the Old Northwest. In the early nineteenth century, the growth of the population of the Midwest took off. By the time of the Civil War, Ohio, Indiana, Illinois, Iowa, Michigan, Wisconsin, Minnesota, Missouri, and Kansas had all become states in the Union.

The culture of these states was essentially that of the East from which most of the settlers came. They were New Englanders and emigrants from the Middle Atlantic States, who spoke English in all matters. The Southerners who entered the territory along the Ohio River route shared the same, mainly British, civilization. In architecture, this meant that they brought late Renaissance styles with them. Settlers from the East Coast remembered the eighteenth-century mode called Georgian, based on the classical ornament derived mainly from studying Roman ruins. Its use in the Midwest was rare, but later classical styles appeared almost at the same time that they did on the East Coast.

Late in the eighteenth century, Scottish brothers Robert Adam (1728–1792) and James Adam (1732–1794) became aware of the excavations at Herculaneum in 1738 and at Pompeii in 1748, both ancient cities buried in a volcanic eruption of Mt. Vesuvius in AD 79. The Adams discovered a different kind of classicism from what previously had been derived from the books of the ancient Roman Vitruvius (first century BC) and Andrea Palladio (1518–1580), the Renaissance Venetian. Instead of the heavy style of Baroque (Georgian) architecture, the Adams developed a lighter, more delicate manner, mainly from their knowledge of paintings at the sites near Naples, that would be dubbed "Adamesque"; in the former American colonies, it would be known as "Federal" for its popularity in the years after the Revolution. It was broadcast from Charleston in South Carolina to Wiscasset in Maine and, of course, marched west with the pioneers.

Shrewsbury House

About the same time that the Adams were expanding the notion of classical architecture, Englishmen James Stuart (1713–1788) and Nicholas Revett (1720–1804) began to publish their studies of ancient Greek architecture, *The Antiquities of Athens* (1762–1830). In spite of the fact that it was well known that classicism had begun with the Greeks, who were imitated by the Romans, few Europeans had gone to the source. Now Stuart and Revett rectified that problem by showing that Greek architecture had a variety of forms from one temple to another. The message was not lost on European and American architects, and a so-called Greek Revival ensued.

Leaders of the movement wished to follow these classical models carefully. Yet their variety encouraged architects to make interpretations that mixed the elements of Greek orders with the somewhat different Roman ones. The return to classical forms offered much opportunity for novelty. What followed was a congeries whose cover-all term might best be called a Classical Revival. Its signature was a temple front, a giant portico often set between two matching wings that exhibited classical detailing such as cornices and egg-and-dart molding. But, especially in American domestic architecture, the classical orders were often simplified so that the only sign of antiquity was a small front porch with its roof supported by two (usually) Ionic columns. Sometimes just a doorway framed at both sides and above the lintel with rectangular lights signaled neoclassicism. The Classical Revival was the dominant style in American domestic architecture between 1830 and 1860.

SMALL TOWN: MADISON, INDIANA

 Jeremiah Sullivan House · 1818 · *Madison, Indiana*

It is difficult to believe that this Federal-style (Adamesque) house was built when Madison had existed only a little more than a decade. In 1818, the town was a settlement of only a few log cabins. Two years later, the census registered 984 residents living in 133 houses. The future looked bright.

Its position on the Ohio River made it an entrepot for people migrating into the Midwest. It was located near the beginning of an Indian trail that led north to Lake Michigan. Gradually improved to make a road (the Michigan Road), this trail became a major route taken by settlers, especially coming from the south, who would move into the interior of the old Northwest Territory. Madison was a staging area for the westward movement and a rival of nearby Cincinnati, which lacked the route to the heartland that Madison inherited from the Indians.

The result was that some citizens of Madison became wealthy by outfitting pioneers for their trip west. By 1820, small industries had been set up to produce goods that would make travel easier. At the same time, the town became a port for shipping livestock downriver to New Orleans. Reveling in its prosperity, it began to be filled with fine houses in the latest styles.

This was the scene when Jeremiah Sullivan, a young lawyer from Virginia, built his Federal-style townhouse. According to authorities, he spurned the temptation to settle in the thriving new cities of Cincinnati or Louisville in order to try his chances in a smaller community. His practice flourished, and he was able to bring his father and mother to Madison. They in turn brought their furniture and fine china with them. These are now on display in various parts of the house.

At the time it was built, it was one of only four brick houses in town. Its fanlighted front door and delicately carved interior woodwork attest to the influence of the Adams on early midwestern architecture. On the other hand, the double chimney is a Georgian survival, evidence of the cultural lag that was common on the frontier. All the details could have been derived from carpenters' handbooks and builders' guides that were available to the aspiring newcomer. The house could easily be fitted into one of the narrow streets of old Alexandria, Virginia.

Sullivan had a successful career as a politician. In 1820, he was elected to the state legislature, and apparently it was his idea to call the Hoosier state's capital Indianapolis. Unfortunately, when he ran for the United States House of Representatives, he lost because, according to one opponent, "he lived in too fine a house."

Sullivan House: the front entrance, the entrance staircase

SULLIVAN HOUSE:
the entrance hall,
the parlor,
the bedroom

JAMES LANIER MANSION · 1840–44 · *Madison, Indiana*
Francis Costigan, architect

In 1836, architect Francis Costigan (1810–1865) came to town. With his distinguished work in public buildings and residences, he raised Madison's architectural significance from a charming village of better-than-average buildings to one with some of the most important Classical Revival structures in America. Yet until John T. Windle, a twentieth-century local historian, bought one of Costigan's most elegant houses and wrote a book on Madison's architecture, Costigan was almost unknown to architectural historians.

Costigan was born in Washington, D.C., and must have absorbed the neoclassicism of Charles Bulfinch and Benjamin Henry Latrobe that was exhibited in the Capitol building and elsewhere. But we do not know anything about his formal training in architecture. In 1835, he was living in Baltimore, and was described in a directory as a "Carpenter and Builder." Again we are left to surmise that he must have moved to Madison because he felt that he might make a place for himself in its burgeoning economy.

His first major commission was the house that he designed for James Lanier, Madison's most successful banker. Although its riverside view sports four two-story columns, it does not have a complete temple front. A pediment is missing, replaced by a fascia board capped on all four sides by anthemions at the middle and at the ends. On the roof is a cupola roughly modeled on the ancient Temple of the Winds in Athens. The effect is splendid. (Note: The wing is obviously late nineteenth century.)

Like many architects in his time, Costigan took the details of the house largely from Minard Lafever's carpenter's handbook *The Beauties of Modern Architecture* (1839) and used them with great assurance. But what is remarkable about the Lanier house and, indeed, the other two houses that we have chosen to be representative is his understanding of the beauty that can be found in a sculpturing of interior space. His ceilings are not just high; his sense of proportion in modeling walls and windows and doors bears comparison to Frank Lloyd Wright's very different approach to spatial arrangement.

Captain Charles Lewis Shrewsbury House · 1846–49 · *Madison, Indiana*

Francis Costigan, architect

Like the nearby Lanier mansion, the smaller house that Costigan designed for Charles Shrewsbury, a merchant, meatpacker, and flour mill owner, brings together all the best attributes of the Classical Revival—the mastery of classical order, the expression of the expansive freedom and nobility of Roman space, and the delight of workmen in rendering elegant classical detail. These make an appeal to the sensitive onlooker.

As you enter, there are two parlors to the left with doubled composite columns separating them. The furniture is not original but is appropriate for the house, having been collected over the years by the present owner, Mrs. Ann Windle, and her late husband, from antiques shops in the eastern United States and Europe. To the right of the front door is a sitting room through which one passes on the way to the dining room. And in the entrance hall is a lovely fifty-three-step spiral staircase down which Shrewsbury unfortunately fell to his death in 1878.

Shrewsbury House: the front entrance, the three-story staircase, spiraling midway to its destination, the two parlors

Francis Costigan House · 1846–49 · *Madison, Indiana*

Francis Costigan, architect

Costigan's own house should have been a subject for *Ripley's Believe It or Not.* Such fine architecture in such a small space, twenty-two feet in width, is surely a miracle of design. The exterior, with its long windows piercing pink brick walls and its elaborate entrance, with its deeply coffered ceiling and its columns in the Composite order, is a remarkably sophisticated interpretation of the Classical Revival.

Costigan House:
the front entrance,
the front entrance (detail),
the dining room

COSTIGAN HOUSE

The house is entered through a tiny hall, with a narrow staircase to the right and an unusually tall curved door to the left leading into a wonderfully proportioned drawing room with a bowed end on the street side. Presumably this was partly work area, but as it stands now, simply furnished, it exhibits beautifully articulated space and attests to the fact that Costigan was an imaginative artist.

(Author's Note: Madison architecture has been well covered in John Windle's *The Early Architecture of Madison, Indiana* [1986]).

Costigan House: the drawing room

Alfred Avery House (the Robbins Hunter Museum) · 1842 · *Granville, Ohio*

Benjamin Morgan, master builder

Alfred Avery was one of the founders of Granville and a successful businessman who naturally wanted his town to proclaim its high culture. In 1842, he hired Benjamin Morgan, a local carpenter, to design and build a house on Broadway, the main street of Granville, that would impress the passersby with his aspirations. Morgan chose a plate in Minard Lafever's popular *The Modern Builder's Guide* and reproduced it almost exactly except for the columns on the side porches. These he copied from those on the Theseum in Athens, which he had seen reproduced in another American carpenter's guide extremely popular on the frontier—Asher Benjamin's *The Builder's Guide* (1839). Both Lafever and Benjamin drew heavily upon James Stuart and Nicholas Revett's *The Antiquities of Athens* and thus form a direct link to British neoclassicism.

Avery House:
the front entrance

Henry B. Clarke House • 1836; additions, 1850, 1872 • *Chicago, Illinois*

Henry B. Clarke was a successful hardware salesman who chose a twenty-eight-acre site at what is now Sixteenth Street and Michigan Avenue in order to build a house. He died in 1849 before the house was finished, but his widow continued the work as funds became available. What we see today was mostly accomplished before 1860. Except for the Italianate cupola added by Mrs. Clarke in the 1850s, the house is yet another variation on the Classical Revival image that can be observed throughout the Midwest. It also is said to be the oldest building in Chicago.

John E. Smith House • 1850 • *Galena, Illinois*

Joseph Smith Jr. House, "the mansion house" • 1842 • *Nauvoo, Illinois*

FOUR

AGE OF CHANGE
1840–1890

The early nineteenth century was a period in which the Classical Revival reigned supreme. Yet the discovery that ancient classicism was not all of one piece, that there were varieties of expression in Greece and Rome, would eventually subvert the notion of a simple, easily recognized order. It would suggest to the classical revivalists that they also, while staying within the classical tradition, might make their own contributions by inventing new decorative devices and substituting them for old ones. The great American classical revivalist Benjamin Henry Latrobe (1764–1820), for example, when designing capitals for columns in the Senate wing of the United States Capitol in Washington, revised the Corinthian order by replacing acanthus leaves with tobacco leaves and corncobs in a patriotic reference to the new country. And he did it with a finesse that Palladio might have admired.

Nevertheless, this expansion of the classical vocabulary was troubling to orthodoxy. Classical discipline was eroding. But even more troublesome was the Gothic Revival that had been waiting in the wings since Wolfgang Goethe, the great German poet, had for the first time spied the Strasbourg cathedral in 1770. Before that, the classically trained man had spurned medieval architecture as barbarous—Gothic! But now he saw the church as resembling a great oak tree whose numerous branches grew irregularly. Nevertheless, when seen as a whole, they suggested a new kind of order, of great complexity, very different from the relatively simple unity of classicism. Goethe, a fervent neoclassicist, later regretted his excess of the spirit, but he had spoken, and he inspired others to enter into what was at first a literary event but later affected all the arts—Romanticism.

In European architecture, the movement led to a reevaluation of Gothic cathedrals and notably in completion of great ones such as that of Cologne. It also inspired the construction of churches based on what were understood to be Gothic principles. Although without any real Gothic monuments, the United States participated in this phenomenon, first of all in religious architecture. For example,

Benjamin Latrobe, previously mentioned as an outstanding classicist, offered the Roman Catholic Bishop of Baltimore two plans for a new cathedral, one classical, the other Gothic. The Bishop chose the former, but Latrobe, probably reasoning that Gothic had always been associated with religion, at first preferred the Gothic version. When asked to design St. Paul's Episcopal Church (1817) in Alexandria, Virginia, he chose Gothic again. It was not built precisely as he had designed it; the ceiling was lowered and his pointed windows on the facade had been replaced by square ones. But from what still exists, his intentions are clear. It was simply a classically designed church with pointed instead of round arches.

Latrobe's confusion of Gothic and classical is significant, for it characterized a good many designs by other church architects in the early nineteenth century. Some went so far as to put round and pointed arches side by side, suggesting that there was a symbolic meaning to the association—probably an allusion to the male and female principles in the Freemasonry that was popular throughout the nineteenth century.

In domestic architecture, the clearest signs of the persistence of classicism is that so many of the so-called Gothic houses are bilaterally symmetrical and based on the typical classical plan—a central hall with staircase and rooms on both sides. Many times, it is only details such as pointed arches and gingerbread bargeboards along the eaves that make them faintly Gothic. Very rarely does medieval imagery appear in the interior spaces. Sometimes a Gothic chair, modeled not on medieval furniture but on the tracery in church windows, ornaments the interiors. But usually the furniture is identical to that used in Classical Revival houses.

Nevertheless, the idea contained in the Gothic Revival view that medieval cathedrals were irregular in outline, sometimes unfinished as at Strasbourg, led in some cases to a revision of the demand for bilateral symmetry. In fact, it opened the way to a freeing up of floor plans and a manipulation of space that would pave the way directly to Frank Lloyd Wright and the Prairie style.

The legitimization of asymmetry led more immediately to the acceptance of another mode—the Italianate or Italian Villa style. Andrew Jackson Downing (1815–1852), an early nineteenth-century horticulturist turned arbiter of taste, argued that though the Americans learned the style from the British, it was a style well developed for the American character. Classical architecture being formal and well balanced, he said, was like George Washington. Gothic architecture, with its flamboyant and picturesque qualities, was like Napoleon. But Americans with their history of compromise might join the styles together in order to have the best qualities of both. The compromise

St. Paul's Episcopal Church • 1817 • *Alexandria, Virginia*
Benjamin Latrobe, architect
Gothic Revival

Curtis-Devin House • 1834 • *Mount Vernon, Ohio*
Gothic Revival

"Wynkook" • 1848 • *Bellevue, Iowa*
Steamboat Gothic

First Presbyterian Church • 1831–32
Kinsman, Ohio
Classical and Gothic Revival

"Litchfield" • 1857 • *Brooklyn, New York*
Alexander Jackson Davis, architect
Italianate

General Ulysses S. Grant House • 1857 • *Galena, Illinois*
Italianate

was the Italianate with its mixture of classical detail and the bold outline of the Gothic. And Downing went on to note that its asymmetry "permits additions, wings, etc., with the greatest facility, and always with increasing effect."

Downing described the Italianate style in his *Architecture of Country Houses* (1850), which was reprinted nine times:

> The leading features of this style are familiar to most of our readers. Roofs rather flat, and projecting upon brackets or cantilevers, windows of various forms, but with massive dressings, frequently running into the round arch, when the opening is an important one . . . , arcades supported on arches or verandas with simple columns, and chimney-tops of characteristic and tasteful forms. Above all when the composition is irregular, rises the campanile or Italian tower, bringing all into unity, and giving picturesqueness, or an expression of power and elevation, to the whole composition.

Downing advised grained woodwork for the interiors, which he noted was more easily kept clean when varnished than when painted. In the least expensive houses, he advised that whitewash should be used on walls, but he preferred wallpaper in various patterns, depending on the whim of the house owner.

> A cornice adds very considerably to the architectural character of any room. . . . Floors should be covered wall-to-wall with carpet, but when the wood is exposed every other plank should be stained a dark color. For those tenants who have the means engravings or plaster casts should decorate at least one room of a house. Curtains and draperies should be hung not only to subdue the glare of sunlight but also for the graceful lines of their folds.

The completeness of his directions for interior design is of great interest to the social historian. I have attempted to simplify a long chapter in Downing's *Country Houses.* He believes that a certain "unity of design" should prevail throughout. It should appear that "it has been produced by a mind working consistently throughout, adjusting and arranging all with a purpose, both of beauty and utility—not by a mind full of odd caprices and whimsical fancies—sometimes producing good effects, and sometimes detestable combinations."

Downing's belief in rational order shows that, well into the period of change, classical principles of beauty were being upheld. These principles would be violated by the end of the nineteenth century, but for the time being they were maintained. As one can see in the images that accompany this text, they held for the mansard-roof (or French Second Empire) style. In fact, its only deviation from the Italian Villa was its huge roof, named for French architect Francois Mansart (1598–1666), a designer of chateaux with enormous roofs with two slopes on each of their four sides, the lower steeper than the upper.

Except for the roof, such houses had all the characteristics of the Italianate, inside and out. Thus, there is no point in describing them further, except to note that this roof had a cultural significance for Americans. In 1852, Napoleon III began an extensive addition to the Louvre, the great Parisian palace that had been converted into an art gallery in the eighteenth century. In building the vast new wings, the architect revived the mansard-style roof. Most Americans would probably not have noticed this phenomenon except that it was precisely at this time that so many of them, beginning with Richard Morris Hunt, began to attend the great architectural school at the École des Beaux-Arts in Paris. The mansard roof entered their palette, signaling a new French influence in American architecture.

GOTHIC REVIVAL

 Dard Hunter House, "Mountain House" · 1850 · *Chillicothe, Ohio*

We have illustrated the variety within the Gothic Revival. Thus, we can justify our choosing an offbeat example of it in order to talk about the genesis of a house that starts out as a peculiar form of Gothic, whose interior was almost totally remodeled by a twentieth-century Arts and Crafts artist in a style new to him—Georgian—and was then filled with mementos of his distinguished life.

The Mountain House is a castellated example of Gothic Revival built in the early 1850s by Louis Meganhoffen, a German emigrant and vintner who proposed to build a mansion that would look down through his vineyard, one of the first in Ohio, toward the Scioto River and the town of Chillicothe. It is a kind of medieval-castle architecture with little attempt to take anything from the Gothic cathedrals. Someone has suggested that the windows on the second-floor level of the towers look like wine bottles and have attributed this touch as an allusion to Meganhoffen's noble profession. Probably they are simply rather awkward attempts at lancet windows influenced by Arab design.

The interior is entirely the work of Dard Hunter, a designer who had joined Elbert Hubbard's Roycroft Arts and Crafts colony in East Aurora, New York, in 1904. According to Janet Ashbee, the wife of the important William Morris–influenced Charles Robert Ashbee, such a designer was needed. Visiting the colony in 1900, she had admired Hubbard's ability to get young people to fashion metal-

DARD HUNTER HOUSE, "MOUNTAIN HOUSE"

work, books, ceramics, and other crafts, but she found that most of their work was barely competent, even ugly. "What the place lacks," she wrote, "is someone with a strong instinct of beauty—who will refuse to pass these inorganic designs and colours that fight. At present they go on the 'do it as well as you can' principle which is very human; but they turn out a lot of poor work." Dard Hunter was the answer to her criticism.

Hubbard hired him, thinking that Hunter, who had training in architecture, could help design the buildings that he intended to construct on the Roycroft campus. But with access to Hubbard's library, Hunter's interest in design took a new turn. He read the *International Studio,* a British publication reprinted with additional material from American sources, which acquainted him with avant-garde movements. He discovered the book designs of William Morris. Perhaps through Morris's work he discovered art glass as well as metalwork. In 1903, on a trip to the West with his brother, a professional magician, he had stayed at the Mission Inn at Riverside, California, and admired the Arts and Crafts furniture there.

His many interests and his ability to carry them out in his designs made him extremely useful to Hubbard, who sent him off to New York to study art-glass design. Then in 1908, Hubbard encouraged him to go to Vienna where he could meet the Austrian masters of the Secessionist movement about whom he had read in the Roycroft library. He left Hubbard in 1910 to be on his own. This took him again to Europe, where he studied lithography. Buttressed by his experience on his father's newspaper, he began experimenting with papermaking. It is not an exaggeration to say that he became one of the world's leading experts and scholars on its production.

Hunter House
"Mountain House:
a side view of the house (p. 37), with castellation, lancet windows, and vineyard terraces,
the entrance hall,
the living room

Hunter House
"Mountain House":
the studio

After successfully opening paper mills in New York and Connecticut, he retired to his hometown and bought the Mountain House. There he established the Mountain House Press that published his books on papermaking. When it came to his remodeling of the interiors of his house, it appears that, except in his studio, he had moved on from Arts and Crafts natural woodwork to Georgian paneling painted white. Whatever the reason for this change of heart, it does show off Hunter's collections of furniture, pictures, and other acquisitions.

The studio, in a wing possibly earlier than the house, looks Arts and Crafts and contains the presses on which Hunter printed his books and other machinery that he used in making paper. Except for Thomas Jefferson's Monticello, no other house in America is so autobiographical.

"American Gothic" House:
the background for Grant Wood's famous painting, an icon representing the Midwest

"American Gothic" House · 1881–82 · *Eldon, Iowa*

Neff Cottage • c. 1830 • *Gambier, Ohio*

Owen Laboratory · 1859 · *New Harmony, Indiana · David Dale Owen, architect, with James Renwick*

Gothic Revival House • c. 1850 • *Marshall, Michigan*

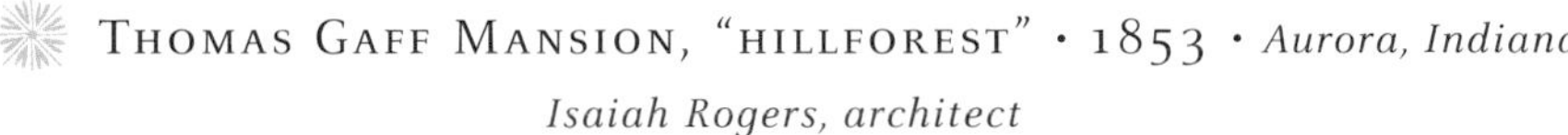

Thomas Gaff Mansion, "hillforest" • 1853 • *Aurora, Indiana*

Isaiah Rogers, architect

Aurora, Indiana, seems like a jumble of the old-bad and the new-bad in architecture today. Still, looking north from the cupola of Hillforest—the mansion that Thomas Gaff built on a hill near the center of town—one can imagine the nineteenth-century community, with its magnificent view of the Ohio River framed by the steeple of the Catholic church, and the tops of trees that now seem to have been planted to screen out the unfortunate trespasses of modern progress. Aurora's reason for being was the river at whose shores docks and warehouses were built that would service the frontiersman and fill up the prairie with emigrants from the eastern states and Europe.

Thomas Gaff (1808–1884) was a Scot who, with his two brothers, James and John, opened a distillery in Philadelphia where the family had settled. At first, he was able to quench the thirst of the Society of Friends (Quakers) and others, and became wealthy very much according to the principles of the American gospel of success. But the Panic of 1837 wiped out the Gaff fortune, and the three men and their families moved west in the early 1840s to Aurora where, in the spirit of American free enterprise, they became active not only in producing spirits but also in investing their newly reconstituted wealth in farms, a foundry, and the construction of turnpikes and canals. They also became active in civic affairs. In 1880, a biographer wrote of Thomas Gaff, "He is generous and ready to relieve the deserving poor. Few men have been more liberal in the contributions to religious and charitable objects."

Gaff Mansion, "Hillforest":
the staircase landing,
the parlor,
the entrance vestibule

The Grotto at Gaff Mansion
"Hillforest"

Gaff Mansion, "Hillforest":
the landscaped gardens,
plan taken from the 1875 *Dearborn County Atlas,* image courtesy of Hillforest Historical Foundation,
the entry hall staircase

His taste was also high. In 1853, he asked Isaiah Rogers, one of the most eminent American architects at that time, to design a mansion for him that would establish his position as an important town father. Rogers, who had an office in nearby Cincinnati, complied with Gaff's request by designing a mansion in the Italianate mode so popular in the mid-century. It has the brackets, long windows with round arched tops, and quoins on the corners of the facade that identify the style, but it is otherwise unique in the history of the Italian villa in America. The front porch with its delicate columns and bowed central pavilion seems more English Regency than Italian.

The decoration of the interior is equally eccentric. A dramatic flying staircase rises from the center of the entry hall. Egyptian motifs surround the several door openings, and the valley of the Nile again appears in the painted palm trees that stand between the painted panels on the walls. The most unusual element in the hall is, however, the parquet floor, dazzling in its design. Unfortunately, it is now heavily carpeted almost wall-to-wall, but pieces of the carpet can be lifted in order to view its intricacies. Surely this room must have been intended for occasional dancing parties.

As you enter, the hall separates the two parlors with their high ceilings and heavy cornices. The dining room is behind the parlor to the left. The upstairs rooms are large but not unusual. Today, they are furnished beautifully and authentically, meaning that they, and indeed all of the rooms in the house, display not only a regard for classical order but also a heaviness of decoration and furnishing that will grow, its high point being in the busy design in the Queen Anne mode of the 1880s.

This tendency to stuff the scene with trivia is also displayed in the proposed design of Hillforest's gardens. The extent of Gaff's cultural uplift program was demonstrated in the proposed landscaping of the grounds, originally ten acres in size. Winding driveways were meant to provide a ceremonial advance to the house. Trees would be distributed in the Victorian manner individually and in clumps with little attention to any order. The plans for floral planting are not known, but the beds undoubtedly would have been filled with colorful specimens. How much of the plan was realized? The present driveways suggest that at least the semblance of the original plan was carried out.

Hillforest was to be set in a typical early Victorian garden. Luckily, a drawing for the plan was made. It was obviously intended to fit the contours of the hill in the "irregular symmetry" demanded by eighteenth-century garden theory, but there are no vistas leading to surprises. Nevertheless, one orthodox garden ornament remains—a small grotto much like a larger one in Alexander Pope's garden at Twickenham.

Needless to say, little remains of this idea of the picturesque; all but a few trees are gone from the main grounds. There are still winding driveways, but they do not seem to follow the system envisioned by the delineator. The long staircase from the front porch to the street continues to intrigue the intrepid climber, but the large vegetable garden to the west was probably never planted, the crest of the hill being too steep. But if you go up into the cupola of the main house, the view of the Ohio River and the forested flatlands of Kentucky beyond suggests the fine living the Gaffs enjoyed.

Abner Pratt House, "Honolulu House"
1860 · *Marshall, Michigan*

Like Madison, Indiana, Marshall flourished in the 1830s and '40s and then went to sleep for a while when other cities were destroying their old buildings in the cause of material progress. In the 1850s, there was a brief awakening when the Michigan Central Railroad came to town, but the removal of its shops in 1874 returned Marshall to somnolence. Perhaps influenced by Rockefeller's restoration of Williamsburg. Harold C. Brooks, a local preservationist, began buying buildings dating from the mid-nineteenth century and restoring them. He even recycled one. Certainly one of the most unusual of these was his own dwelling, the Honolulu House. It rates as one of America's greatest and most welcome follies.

Bearing a slight resemblance to the Iolani Palace (1882) in Honolulu, this house is a lot older (1860) and a lot more Hawaiian. Both are basically Italianate buildings. The Honolulu House was built by Abner Pratt, the first American Consul to Hawaii (1857–1859), who on returning to Marshall decided to build a house that would evoke the spirit of Polynesia. For him, this meant a pagoda-roofed central tower under which lay a porch of lyrical ogee arches and outsized brackets.

The interior was redone in 1887, but the Hawaiian theme was sustained particularly in the wall paintings by F. A. Grace, which feature tropical scenes. All this has been beautifully restored and is open to the public.

PRATT HOUSE, "HONOLULU HOUSE"

Octagon House · c. 1856 · *Barrington, Illinois*

Orson Squire Fowler (1809–1887), whose book *The Octagon House: A Home For All* (1848) introduced Americans to the novel house type, was born in Cohocton in upper New York State, an area that produced more than its share of eccentrics in the mid-nineteenth century. His parents were New Englanders. He went to Amherst College, where his best friend was Henry Ward Beecher, the brother of Harriet Beecher Stowe, the author of *Uncle Tom's Cabin.* While at Amherst, Fowler and Beecher fell into a study of phrenology, the pseudo science of reading a person's health and character by studying the contours of his head. After their graduation in 1834, Beecher became a famous preacher, but Fowler made a life's work of publishing essays and lecturing on phrenology.

We know him for his book on houses. Like many Victorians, Fowler looked to nature for models of good living and noted the frequency of the circle in plant life. Accommodated to then-current building techniques, he determined that the circle should be regularized so that it would have eight sides. Compared to the usual rectangular house plan, space would be conserved and dark corners would be eliminated. He also believed that it would be easier to heat in the winter and to keep cool in the summer.

It is estimated that about 3,000 octagon houses were built more or less following Fowler's plan. He suggested that they be constructed in concrete, but most were actually built in brick or wood frame. Even though present-day discussions of octagon houses emphasize the fact that few were built, the wonder is that they caught on at all. Almost all of the old states in the Union have them, most dating from the 1850s. They offer a refreshing variation on the common house.

Situated on the edge of the business district, this house has been converted to office space. The exterior, however, preserves the Italianate brackets, long windows, and the wraparound porch that we associate with the typical octagon house.

FRENCH SECOND EMPIRE (MANSARD)

Iowa Governor's Mansion, "Terrace Hill" · 1867–69 · *Des Moines, Iowa*

William W. Boyington, architect

Located on one of the hills overlooking the city of Des Moines, Iowa, Terrace Hill is an exuberant Italianate pile dominated by a ninety-foot-high tower capped with a mansard roof. It is what we call French Second Empire and deserves to be compared to the Missouri governor's mansion (pp. 58–63) built just a few years later at taxpayers' expense. Terrace Hill was designed by one of Chicago's earliest architects, William W. Boyington (1818–1898), for a wealthy Des Moines businessman, Benjamin F.

Iowa Governor's Mansion
"Terrace Hill":
the front entrance,
the main stairway

Allen. Boyington is best known for his Gothic Revival–style Chicago Water Tower and Pumping Station (1867–69) which was one of the few buildings in downtown Chicago to survive the great fire of 1871.

Benjamin F. Allen had made his fortune in commerce and banking and is said to have been Iowa's first millionaire. He built the house in order to signal his economic status in the community, but bad luck in his wild speculative adventures in the 1870s forced him to sell it to Frederick M. Hubbell, another speculator who had made his money in insurance and real estate. There, Hubbell was able to stage lavish parties and to marry his daughter into Swedish nobility.

As is usual in most museum houses, the furniture is not original for the most part, but it is well selected to evoke the times in which the house was built. There is more furniture than exists in the Missouri governor's mansion, which gives the rooms a generally busy feeling, but as in the latter, the high ceilings create a space that prevents claustrophobia.

The house was given to the state in 1971 by the Hubbell family.

Iowa Governor's Mansion "Terrace Hill": the mantelpiece, the dining room, the library

Missouri Governor's Mansion • 1871 • *Jefferson City, Missouri*

George Ingham Barnett, architect

Jean Carnahan has published a book titled *If the Walls Could Talk: The Story of Missouri's First Families* (1998), a coupling of the history of the governor's mansion with the lives of the people who lived in it. Her method brings out many a good and often significant story. For the architectural historian, it gives insight into the many changes that have been made to the house since it was built in 1871. Almost every first lady found it wanting in some respects and attempted to improve it, so much so that it is a miracle that it has retained its character.

The architect of the house was George Ingham Barnett (1815–1898), an Englishman who had the usual British architectural training in an architect's office in London. In 1839, he decided to try his fortune in the United States; he left England to work a few months in New York and then moved west to St. Louis. He had a distinguished career in both public and domestic architecture, where he established himself as an enthusiast for the French Second Empire (mansard) style, the style of the governor's mansion. Considering his background in England, his choice of this style was rather strange, for there are few mansard roofs in Britain. But like other architects, he catered to the style of the times, and in 1870s America, that was French Second Empire.

The house was built during the short administration of B. Gratz Brown (1826–1885), another St. Louis product, a newspaper editor with pretensions to the presidency of the United States. In 1872, he settled for the vice presidency on the losing Liberal Republican ticket with Horace Greeley. Elected to the Missouri governorship in 1871, he took a great interest in building the mansion. He helped to plan it and, in fact, donated four Missouri red granite columns quarried from his property in Iron County to be the support for the roof of the entrance portico. On their arrival, Gratz noticed that they had been cut a few inches too short, so he simply had the spaces filled in with white stone bases that to this day add interest to the entrance. He also bought two huge chandeliers for the parlors. He was appalled at their price of $150 apiece but finally relented and accepted them.

The house cost $75,000. It is sixty-six feet square with large bay windows at each end of the pink brick building. The entrance hall is seventeen feet high. Off it to the left is a library and beyond that an elegant staircase. On the other side is a double parlor and to the rear is a large dining room. The kitchen, once in the basement, is now in an addition erected in the 1930s in a major face-lift. There are seven spacious bedrooms upstairs, and a ballroom and a few bedrooms are on the third floor under the mansard roof.

Missouri Governor's Mansion: the entrance hall

The original building had no closets or bathrooms. As the governors came and went, their wives directed their attention to correcting these imperfections, but a parsimonious state legislature often cut off funds for the upkeep of the house, and the women had to plead with the lawmakers. That usually meant they had to make do with the pittance that was provided. A good case could be made for adding closets and bathrooms, but furniture, draperies, carpets, and wallpaper were minor considerations for legislators who believed that enough money had been expended on simply building a mansion of noble proportions. Maintenance and improvement were minor matters.

A major restoration was begun in 1974 under the direction of another governor's wife, Carlyn Bond, and restoration architect Ted Wofford. Mrs. Bond advertised for donations of furniture appropriate to the 1870s and even received some of the original furnishings. She also secured a bond issue that raised nearly two million dollars for the restoration of the entire house. Today, under the watchful eye of Mary Pat Abele, who was hired by Mrs. Bond to supervise the state of the house and public tours, the executive mansion looks splendid and, even though on a smaller scale, is worthy of comparison to Queen Victoria's Italianate Osbourne House on the Isle of Wight.

Missouri Governor's Mansion:
the front entrance,
the front parlor

Missouri Governor's Mansion:
the entrance hall,
looking toward
the back parlor,
the staircase

QUEEN ANNE

So far, we have seen a weakening of the classical tradition but not a rejection of it. The physical representation of the Classical Revival ended at about the time of the Civil War (1861–1865), but the esthetic, the adherence to order though of a different kind, prevailed. The Queen Anne style of the 1880s certainly threatened that order: fanciful facades leaving no place to rest the eye, interiors with rugs scattered across inlaid hardwood floors, and wallpaper designs swearing at each other. This marked a break with neoclassicism—but, as we shall see, not a final break.

The Queen Anne style was another British import. Its chief advocate, Richard Norman Shaw, saw it as a return to the English country house tradition of the landed aristocracy even though his nineteenth-century clients were mainly businessmen and not earls. More Jacobean than Queen Anne, it was an architecture of high peaked roofs, gables, red brick, tiles, and asymmetry. Picked up by Americans, it was translated into wood shingles and stucco with torrents of gingerbread and contrasts in paint, often green and red. The interiors were garish and filled with things. Everywhere there were objects covering every square inch of flat surface.

How did this happen? Basically, it was a matter of the bourgeoisie competing with each other in a spectacular demonstration of what Thorstein Veblen, the American economist, called "conspicuous consumption." It was also a reflection of a vogue of Japan that seized the Western world after Admiral Perry set anchor at the bay of Yokohama in 1854. The American reaction, except for a pride in having an American ship opening up the hermit kingdom, was not immediate. It was for the Europeans to capitalize esthetically on the American discovery of Japan's exotic culture. A vogue of Japan affected painting, music, drama, architecture, and interior design.

When the Civil War ended, the Americans took up the vogue of Japan with at least as much enthusiasm as the British and French. They entered what was called an "esthetic movement." But instead of imitating Japanese restraint, the Americans used Japanese art to fill up their houses. Japanese pots (usually imitations) appeared everywhere. As a matter of fact, the discovery of Japanese art pottery encouraged the development of American ceramics, such as that produced by Rookwood in Cincinnati and Pewabic in Detroit. And the products of these kilns were spread everywhere.

A new profession arose out of the Queen Anne craze of the 1880s—interior design. By all odds, the most important of the interior designers was Charles Locke Eastlake (1836–1906), whose book *Hints on Household Taste,* published in England in 1868 and in the United States in 1872, was intended to discipline the tendency toward excessive ornament that was already sweeping the English-speaking world. Whatever its many faults, industrialism had raised the standard of living and provided leisure time in which people could focus on the state of their homes. Eastlake encouraged the acquisition of books, sculpture, and other art objects in moderation and good taste, and coupled this advice with a moral message, a practice dear to the Victorian mind. "Sincere" furniture would save many a marriage, he thought. He hated tables with "gouty" legs and advocated "honesty" in all ornaments. Although his message was directed at discipline, its emphasis on good design actually encouraged Victorians to collect more and more stuff.

Charles Hackley House · 1887–89 · *Muskegon, Michigan*

David S. Hopkins, architect

If ever a house expressed the enigma of the American businessman, this is it. Go up the outside stairs at the front of the house and enter a hall filled with symbolic figures—human heads, monkeys, dogs, cherubs—carved into the woodwork. Charles Hackley would not have understood the symbolism, but he would be proud of its ostentation. It is an unnerving room, but it is nevertheless impressive, intended to overwhelm the visitor who would probably never see any other room in the house. Busy is the word. Once encountered, this room is never forgotten.

In a sense, it screens the person that Hackley was: quiet, unassuming, always shaded from the limelight. After leaving school at the age of fifteen, he had entered his father's construction business, and after his father's death in 1874, he used his inheritance to form the C. H. Hackley Lumber Company in Muskegon, in 1881, he went into a business partnership with Thomas Hume, an Irish emigrant. Together they built an exceptional lumber business and, when the Michigan forests were overcut in the late nineteenth century, they bought into other industries and encouraged them to relocate in Muskegon, thereby assuring a secure economic base for the city. His understanding of business opportunity paid off. At the time of his death in 1905, he had secured a fortune of more than twelve million dollars.

Hackley House: the dining room, detail, the front entrance and outbuildings (pp. 66–67), the chimney flue with Islamic window inset (p. 67)

HACKLEY HOUSE

Hackley House: a bedroom, the entrance hall

Hackley was strongly influenced by the ideas of Andrew Carnegie, the steel magnate, who observed in his *Gospel of Wealth* (1889) that "[a] man who dies rich dies disgraced." In the latter part of his life, he spent his vast fortune endowing public libraries, teachers' pensions, and other good works. Hackley followed him by building and endowing a public library, a hospital, a manual-training school, and a park. He even spent money on sculpture so that the people of Muskegon could associate themselves with the lives of famous men.

Hackley heeded Carnegie's admonition that the successful businessman's home should in its quality "serve as an inspiration" to the general public. His architect, David S. Hopkins, a resident of Grand Rapids, deployed all the devices that the Queen Anne mode suggested—clapboard siding, a corner tower, tall sculptured brick chimneys, and Chinese moon gates on a balcony above the wraparound front porch. The exterior ensemble was trimmed in the manner, wrongly attributed as it turned out, to Charles Locke Eastlake, the English interior designer whose *Hints on Household Taste* was the primer for Americans uneasy about their ability to discern the difference between the good and bad in decorating and furnishing their houses. We have come to call this trim used on both the interior and exterior of houses "gingerbread" for its excessive ornamentation. The stenciled ceilings and elaborate woodwork crafted by skilled workmen for the Kelly Brothers Manufacturing Company of Muskegon is equally jarring.

Hackley shared the elaborate onion-domed stables with his old partner, Thomas Hume, who had built a house next door. Even though Hume's house was designed by Hackley's architect and was built at the same time, it is in fact larger than the Hackley house. It is much simpler in its interior detail and in places anticipates the much more reticent Shingle style and Arts and Crafts interiors that were to follow in the 1890s.

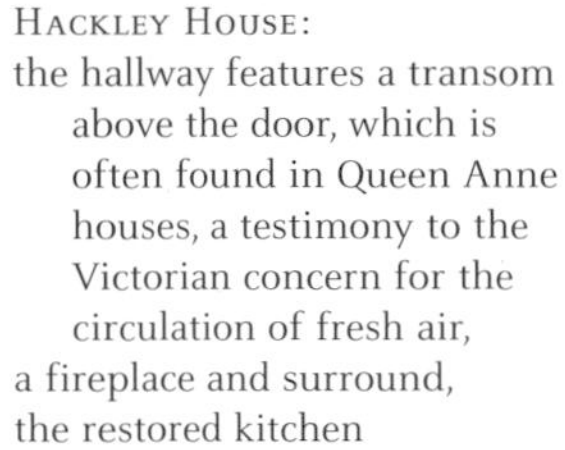

Hackley House:
the hallway features a transom above the door, which is often found in Queen Anne houses, a testimony to the Victorian concern for the circulation of fresh air,
a fireplace and surround,
the restored kitchen

HACKLEY HOUSE

William Thomas Proudfoot House, "Hillside Cottage" • 1881

Wichita, Kansas • Proudfoot and Bird, architects

William Thomas Proudfoot (1860–1928) and George Washington Bird (1854–1953) designed this small building shortly after they formed their partnership. It was Proudfoot's own residence. Even though it is small by Victorian standards, it bears a strong resemblance to the much larger Watts Sherman House (1874–76) in Newport, Rhode Island, usually attributed to the great Boston architect, H. H. Richardson. The stone base, the window treatment, the decorative effect of the horizontal panels with their vertical strips of wood, the shingles—all these constructions suggest early Richardsonian domestic architecture strongly affected by the Queen Anne style of Richard Norman Shaw in England.

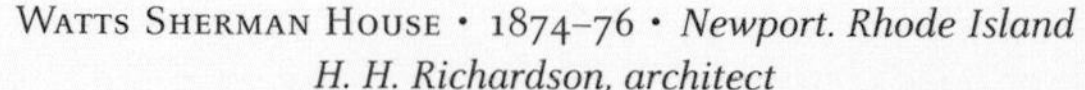

Watts Sherman House • 1874–76 • *Newport. Rhode Island*
H. H. Richardson, architect

PROUDFOOT HOUSE, "HILLSIDE COTTAGE"

Both Proudfoot and Bird would have had knowledge of the work of Richardson and may even have seen published drawings of the Watts Sherman house. As a young man, Bird lived in Philadelphia, where he is supposed (his background is sketchy) to have belonged to the T-Square Club, a group of young architects, including Wilson Eyre (see Freer House, pp. 79–83), who had Beaux-Arts training and were also interested in the Arts and Crafts movement. Proudfoot was trained in the office of the Des Moines firm of Foster and Liebe, and then, probably in 1884–85, spent a short period of time at MIT, then only a block from Richardson's Trinity Church in Boston. That Proudfoot and Bird were both familiar with Richardson is apparent in their Wichita City Hall (1892), which is pure (and wonderful) Richardsonian Romanesque. Even though it is in a totally different style from Proudfoot's "Hillside Cottage," it and several other Wichita buildings torn down in the urban renewal craze of the 1960s demonstrate their appreciation and understanding of Richardson's work.

Forced into bankruptcy in the financial turmoil of 1892, Proudfoot and Bird moved their office to Salt Lake City and then to Des Moines. Bird retired to California in 1912, but Proudfoot reconstituted the firm. Under the name Proudfoot, Bird and Rawson, it developed the largest practice in the state of Iowa in the early twentieth century.

Proudfoot House
"Hillside Cottage":
the hallway and stairs

Clement Studebaker House • 1889

South Bend, Indiana • Henry Ives Cobb, architect

Henry Ives Cobb (1859–1931) was a prominent Chicago architect with a fine pedigree. After spending a year at MIT, he enrolled in the Lawrence Scientific School at Harvard where he received a degree in 1881. Cobb was employed immediately by the Boston architectural firm of Peabody and Stearns; the same year, he received an independent commission from the Union League Club in Chicago to design a building for them. Like many ambitious New Englanders, he decided to move to Chicago, where he received many lucrative commissions for domestic as well as public buildings. He designed a neo-Gothic mansion for the Potter Palmers and a Shingle-style church for the Presbyterians of Lake Forest, but he seemed to prefer the Romanesque style that H. H. Richardson had made famous by now. His Fisheries Building at the World's Columbian Exposition was a fanciful episode in that style.

It seems probable that Cobb had seen Richardson's John G. Glessner Mansion (1886–87) in Chicago before he convinced Clement Studebaker, the carmaker, that the Romanesque style was appropriate for an industrial giant. The Studebaker house, while formidable, does not have the tight design that makes the street facade of Richardson's Glessner house memorable. It is mainly cobblestones and has plenty of Syrian arches. The porte cochere is grand and must have impressed visitors driving up to it. Furthermore, the house is carefully designed from all sides, which is more than can be said about the Glessner mansion, whose inner courtyard is bizarre. The Studebaker House is now a restaurant.

John G. Glessner Mansion
1886–87 • *Chicago, Illinois*
H. H. Richardson, architect

FIVE

AGE OF REFORM

SHINGLE STYLE

Charles Lang Freer House · 1887–90 · *Detroit, Michigan*

Wilson Eyre, architect

To most of us, the name Freer is associated with an art museum that is on the mall in Washington, D.C. Although it includes all of Charles Lang Freer's distinguished collection of Asian art, the exhibit that attracts the most art lovers is the so-called "Peacock Room" that James McNeill Whistler had created for Frederick R. Leyland, a wealthy London shipowner, in 1876–77; Freer purchased it in 1904 and had it installed in the carriage house behind his mansion in Detroit. After Freer's death, it was given to the museum that bears his name.

Freer (1856–1919) was a successful businessman who had made his fortune in manufacturing railroad freight cars; in fact, he was so successful that he was able to retire at the age of forty-five to pursue his passion for Asian art, contemporary American art, and the products of Detroit's own Pewabic Pottery. By 1890, his collection was so vast that he needed a large house to contain it. He employed the highly respected Philadelphia architect Wilson Eyre (1858–1944) to design the house that architectural historian Vincent Scully Jr. would call the Shingle style, related to the Queen Anne style but without the gingerbread.

Perhaps influenced by the Japanese Zen Buddhist search for simplicity, Freer chose Eyre over his friend Stanford White, possibly because he was afraid of White's tendency to render grandeur. Though he designed many mansions, Eyre had an interest in Japanese understatement, as did Freer. Eyre created a low-key facade that is subdued, though picturesque and impressive in its contrast of the hard blue limestone of the first floor with gray shingles above it. It is disciplined by classical symmetry with a central pavilion flanked by almost identical wings. Two tall chimneys, holdovers from the Queen Anne style, frame the house.

Freer House

Freer House:
the upper hallway
(pp. 78–79),
a bay window,
the front entrance

The reticence is carried inside in the elegance of the stair hall, which is placed at the rear of the entrance hall. The delicate staircase is a far cry from Stanford White's heavy monumentality. The effect is achieved with a wooden balustrade filled in with carved panels suggesting interlaced strips of bamboo, a sure sign of Asian influence. This leads to a gallery of lyric arches. At the front of the house is an impressive entrance hall. The other rooms are clustered around this central space. The art gallery is upstairs.

FREER HOUSE:
an exterior detail,
viewed from the rear courtyard,
a back door and window (detail),
leading onto the rear courtyard,
a fireplace surround,
framed with Pewabic tiles

In the Japanese manner, Freer entertained guests by bringing out items from his collection to be contemplated and admired—then put away. The walls were hung with a few pictures from his collection of contemporary American artists such as Dwight Tryon, Thomas Dewing, Abbott Thayer, and John Singer Sargent. Today these works of art are at the Freer Gallery of Art in Washington, D.C., and the house, now used for offices, seems underfurnished. Perhaps that is just as well for it is possible to see its fine architecture more clearly.

C. G. Conn House • 1874; c. 1910 • *Elkhart, Indiana*

Excuse me for using the first person singular, but I have a special place in my heart for this house. When I was four years old, it was just around the corner from the house where my family lived on Lexington Avenue. A few days after we moved in, my mother took my brother and me on a walk around the block and, according to her story, when we saw the Conn house, my brother observed, "It's a shursh," and I corrected him, "No, it's an ibary." The incident became one of her favorite stories.

It is, of course, a fine example of what was called Beaux-Arts at the turn of the nineteenth century. The core of the house was built in 1874 by Samuel Strong, an Elkhart banker who followed up by renaming the street for himself. But the visual treat is the grand Corinthian colonnade that C. G. Conn (1844–1931), a band instrument manufacturer, added to it around 1910. No one seems to know who the architect was.

It is unusual to find a truly Beaux-Arts house. The classical colonnade, expressing its debt to the World's Columbian Exposition of 1893, was normally associated with public architecture—city halls, banks, libraries, auditoriums—often set formally in planned civic centers. Probably Conn had been to the Chicago fair and had been impressed by its magnificence. The Conn house certainly is an unexpected display of the grandiose on a street of rather conventional houses.

According to the story, Conn, a veteran of the Civil War, got into a fight with one of his fellow soldiers, who punched him so hard in the mouth that his lips were damaged and he could not play his cornet. But he overcame the painful experience of putting metal to his lips by inventing a rubber mouthpiece. After the war was over, he capitalized on his invention. Apparently, many horn players appreciated the comfort of the rubber mouthpieces. Conn was so successful at selling them that he expanded his hobby by creating the musical instruments

Conn House:
the exterior mosaic floor,
the front entrance

behind them. He built a factory near the St. Joseph River (in Elkhart it is known as the St. Joe) and soon turned the city into the band instrument capital of the world—Buescher horns, Leedy drums, Selmer clarinets, and Conn tubas and trumpets.

My association with Conn did not end with my early childhood. In 1929, we moved to another house on the banks of St. Joe. It was only a few blocks from the Conn factory, which I passed every weekday on my way to Beardsley School. The facade of the factory was pure Mission Revival. We lived next door to Carl D. Greenleaf, who took over the company in 1915. He and his wife, Deacon, were among my father and mother's friends. Their house, now demolished, was another Beaux-Arts mansion.

Conn House:
the living room, hallway, and dining room,
the enclosed second-floor porch

J. Sterling Morton and Carolyn Joy House, "Arbor Lodge" • 1855–1903

Nebraska City, Nebraska

Nebraska City today is a quiet Missouri River town. When J. Sterling Morton (1832–1902) and his bride arrived in town in 1855, it was a trading post—loose, free, and full of gunslingers. It was also a station on the Underground Railroad in the period before the Civil War. Here fugitive slaves from Missouri and the Southern states were prepared by John Brown and his followers to find freedom in Canada. The coming of the railroad in 1871, supplanting the traffic on the river, quieted down Nebraska City. It is now a "site of" town with few shards of its early history remaining.

When the Mortons arrived seven years before the Homestead Act (1862), they asserted their squatter's right to a strip of rich loess overlooking the river and the Iowa bluffs. Although there were trees along the river, the Mortons' property was virtually treeless, as was most of the land on the prairie. Thereby hangs a tale. Being easterners (Sterling from New York and Carolyn Joy from Chicago), the Mortons did not share the early pioneers' notion of the forest as the enemy of civilization. Far from it—they longed for trees and began to plant them on their estate. The result is a plantation of great interest for its age and variety of species. It follows that when Morton became president of the Nebraska Board of Agriculture, he proclaimed a day of tree planting—the first Arbor Day, April 10, 1874.

Although he began his Nebraska experience by becoming editor of the *Nebraska City News*, his interest, besides trees, lay in politics. Shortly after his arrival, he was elected to the Nebraska territory's second legislative assembly. Having spotted Morton as a valuable Democrat, President James Buchanan appointed him acting governor of the Nebraska Territory, an office that he held until 1867 when Nebraska became a state.

For a time Morton turned his attention to agriculture. He became interested in farm improvement and was involved in soil conservation programs. Then in 1893, President Grover Cleveland chose him to be in his cabinet as Secretary of Agriculture. After four years in that office, he returned to Nebraska City, where he published a weekly journal called *The Conservative*. He also drastically expanded the house that he and Carolyn had built in 1855 to a fifty-two-room mansion decked out in Beaux-Arts neoclassicism.

It is a sophisticated design, well beyond the skills of a local architect. It may remind you of the White House in Washington and suggest that Morton had aspirations for the U.S. presidency. Whatever its meaning, it is outwardly a fine example of Beaux-Arts architecture. The interior, except for a grand staircase in the Beaux-Arts tradition, is disappointing architecturally. Nonetheless, the Nebraska memorabilia that it holds is fascinating.

MORTON HOUSE, "ARBOR LODGE"

Ferdinand and Emily Tomek House · 1907 · *Riverside, Illinois*

Frank Lloyd Wright, architect

One of Wright's early Prairie-style houses, the Tomek House demonstrates all the powers of design that Wright had developed through a period beginning in the 1880s. In a sense, it is the only example of the houses we have studied thus far where the architect makes an attempt to let the house reflect the peculiar qualities of the landscape in which it is sited—the prairie. The horizontal lines on which it is based reflect the relatively flat land around it. But we should be careful about attributing too much environmentalism to his work. After all, he built Prairie-style houses in Rochester, New York, and in the hills of Montecito, California, both cities far from the prairie. Also, horizontality appeared in the design

Tomek House:
the dining room and hallway,
the side entrance

TOMEK HOUSE

of Wright's contemporaries—Bernard Maybeck in the San Francisco area and the brothers Charles and Henry Greene in Pasadena.

The beauty of the horizontal was its broader interpretation. It allowed Wright's buildings to seem to merge with the landscape and to anchor them to the ground upon which they were constructed. The horizontal was also a factor in bringing together the elements of their interiors in an organic relationship. It was part of Wright's mastery of the fundamentals of sculpturing space so that one room flows into another almost imperceptibly. Steps down into a living room increase the sensation of an explosion of space. Changes in floor plan result in an experience very like that felt in an English eighteenth-century landscape garden—surprise. So good was Wright at mastering the fundamentals of space, it was as if he had invented them himself. In fact, his spaces were different from those of all previous architects and all

Tomek House:
the living room,
flanked by two hallways

his contemporaries, including Greene & Greene and Bernard Maybeck. Indeed, his own students in the Prairie style found it difficult to master his sense of space.

The entry to the Tomek House is through a door at ground level, where a short flight of stairs rises to the major living space. Bedrooms were always a nuisance to Wright, who believed that the main purposes of a house were social. He tucked them away in a small attic story that included one bath. The lower (first) floor contains the living and dining areas, connected by a hall with a dropped ceiling so that both rooms break from the hall into vertical space. The dining room is otherwise conventional, but the living room centers on a dominant fireplace, a Wrightean symbol of the sanctity of the family who would gather around it in the evening for conversation or music as it did at the two Taliesins, his homes in Scottsdale, Arizona, and Spring Green, Wisconsin.

John B. and Amelia Franke House · 1914 · *Fort Wayne, Indiana*

Barry Byrne, architect

As a teenager, Barry Byrne (1883–1967) was drawn to Frank Lloyd Wright's architecture. With a humble Irish-Catholic background, he left parochial school at the age of fourteen in order to work in the mail order rooms of Montgomery Ward in Chicago. One Sunday in 1902, on one of his regular trips to the Chicago Art Institute, he happened on an exhibit of Wright's architecture and was thrilled by it, so much so that he took the trolley out to Oak Park and asked Wright for a job in his office. Wright, who had little formal education himself and was thus sympathetic to this young man, took him in.

Franke House: the front elevation, the living room

FRANKE HOUSE

FRANKE HOUSE: the living room, the bathroom sink, the organ console and music rolls

Byrne was a quick learner and was soon involved in Wright's early commissions, including the Unity Temple in Oak Park, which introduced him to the design of religious architecture, a subject that would interest him to the end of his life. But his early independent work was in Prairie-style houses, first in the Seattle area in a partnership with Andrew Willatzen, another Wright protégé. Their major commissions were in domestic architecture and in the Wrightean manner. Byrne returned to Chicago in 1913, when Walter Burley Griffin, yet another Wright apprentice, went off to Australia and asked Byrne to manage his office. It was during this period that Byrne produced his best Prairie-style buildings, including the John and Amelia Franke House.

John Franke, who made his fortune in the pastry industry (Perfection Biscuits), delighted in gadgets, and they are distributed throughout the house. Few of them work anymore, including the 400-stop pipe organ with which he entertained the neighbors with concerts through open windows; it must be restored, for the house came with hundreds of rolls of recorded organ music.

The house has other unusual features such as a mural of Adam and Eve in the Garden of Eden, Adam hoeing and Eve reaching for the forbidden fruit. The artist Alfonso Iannelli, who worked for Wright and other Prairie-school architects, painted Adam and Eve in the nude. This was too much for Amelia Franke, who had Iannelli clothe them respectably. Pity!

Byrne's understanding of Wrightean sculpture of space shines through the interior of this building. Few of Wright's talented contemporaries—including Marion Mahoney, Walter Burley Griffin, and William Gray Purcell and George Grant Elmslie—mastered this aspect of Wright's genius. Barry Byrne is the exception. But even with great photography, the interiors cannot be fully enjoyed. You have to be there.

Foursquare House · c. 1910 · *Barrington, Illinois*

Foursquare House:
a structure typical of
thousands in the Midwest

William Allen and Sallie Lindsay White House, "red rocks" • 1920–21

Emporia, Kansas • Wight and Wight, architects

Only a few people who were born after 1920 have the slightest idea of who William Allen White was. Those who do, one wagers, live in Emporia. But in his day, he was one of the most famous literary figures in the country. In 1895, at the age of twenty-seven, he bought the *Emporia Gazette* and, as owner, publisher, and editor, turned this small town Populist paper into one of the most quoted newspapers in the United States. Most of the quotations were from his writing.

White was a Liberal Republican, a species now almost extinct. A friend of Teddy Roosevelt, he was one of the liberals who pulled out of the Republican Party in 1912 in order to found the Progressive ("Bull Moose") Party that chose Roosevelt as their candidate for president. White was also a close friend of Clarence Darrow, the cheeky young lawyer who defended John Scopes in the famous "Monkey Trial" that tested Tennessee's laws against the teaching of evolution in public schools.

But for architectural historians, his most significant friend was Frank Lloyd Wright. The friendship apparently began when White wrote to Wright in 1915, asking him to "do over" Red Rocks, his Queen Anne mansion. He was afraid that Wright might turn him down,

> . . . for our house is one of those old fashioned houses, warted all over with bow windows, and towers and gables and fibroid tumors, acute angles, meaning nothing and merely serrating the skyline. It is chopped up into all sorts of little rooms and cubbyholes and senseless little dabs of space. . . . Yet it is our house and the children were born here and there is a certain sentiment in having lived in a place 16 years, when that 16 years is the core of your life and happiness, and we have an animal fear of being turned out of the house into a new house.

Wright was charmed and began work on the designs for remodeling. A long series of letters and visits from Wright ensued. But as their friendship deepened, White's enthusiasm waned into concern that what Wright was envisioning was too radical for Emporia and for the Whites. Even though Wight and Wight, the Kansas City firm that finally remodeled the house, apparently used several of Wright's ideas, Wright did not complain. Indeed, the friendship became deeper. In his moving eulogy of White, Wright recalled the many times the "Taliesin Boys" stopped off in Emporia on their trips between Spring Green and Scottsdale and indulged themselves in Sallie White's fine cooking.

The Wight and Wight transformation of the house into a Tudor villa came out well. But seeing the Wright drawings makes one a little sad that the master of the Prairie style never got a chance to have at the "warts" and "fibroid tumors" of the original Queen Anne style of the White house.

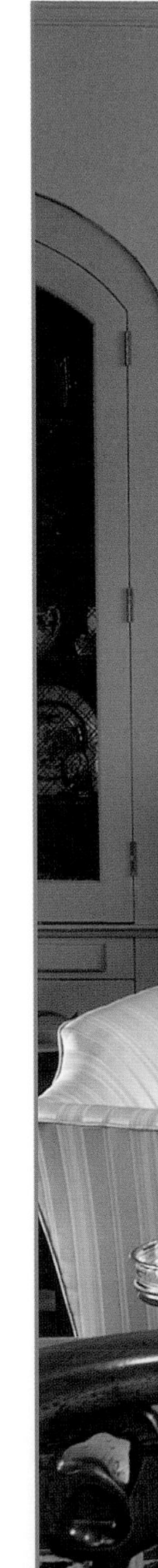

John L. and Florence N. Evans House · 1930 · *Wichita, Kansas*
William Henry Lautz, architect

In the 1920s, Southern Californians chose the Spanish farmhouse as a model for their residential architecture. Midwesterners, on the other hand, mainly skirted the Spanish image and in great numbers chose the Tudor mode as their favorite period revival.

Evans House: the living room

Evans House:
the bathroom,
the front entrance

EVANS HOUSE

The fine residential areas of Wichita are full of Tudor Revival houses, many of them well designed, as is the Evans House. Its architect was William Henry Lautz (1893–1973), who received his BA in architecture from the Armour Institute of Technology (now the Illinois Institute of Technology) in 1913. Lautz taught architecture at the Armour Institute; in fact, he had Louis Sullivan lecture to his classes. His architectural practice was mainly in Chicago's South Side, at that time an upper-class community. But the Great Depression of the 1930s did him in. He never practiced architecture again.

Lautz designed the house for his sister-in-law, Florence Evans. The tall Tudor gable with its black-and-white work dominates the facade, which remains today exactly as it was when it was built in 1930. But it is the interiors with their original colors intact and much of the Evans's furniture still in use that sets the house apart from the usual 1920s mansions that have often been modernized by new tenants.

The present owner, a member of the Evans family, has preserved the spirit of the twenties and at the same time has added to it her own deep interest in the Arts and Crafts movement, past and present. She has used William Morris wallpaper and fabrics in various places in the house. Her collection of ceramics is exceptional.

CHICAGO BUNGALOW

There are about 80,000 bungalows in the Chicago area, most of them dating from the 1920s. They look different from their California relatives. First and foremost, the Chicago variety is rarely shingled. One misses the ability of the West Coast product to merge with its natural surroundings. In fact, the Chicago bungalow with its typically tiny front yard had little room for trees. There was limited space for a garden in the backyard. The style is different, too. While the California bungalow shows Tudor, Swiss Chalet, as well as Japanese influences, the Chicago bungalow is all but nondescript except that quite a few of them show a Prairie-style connection.

Chicago bungalows often feature art glass, particularly in the front windows, some of it very beautiful. Also, most of them are made of brick and are often noteworthy for the way they display the mason's art. Their facades are usually covered with "face brick," very different from the common brick used on the other sides of the house. It has a variety of patterned color that gives texture to the building. Typically, in California, the lots were around fifty feet in width. In Chicago, the lots were twenty-five to thirty-seven feet wide, reflecting the higher value of the land in an already populous city.

The California bungalow also experienced growing pains. The expansive ones were built in the period before World War I when land was relatively cheap. After the war, developers built bungalows in tracts just as they did in Chicago, and they had to fit them into smaller spaces. But the Chicago bungalow was almost always narrower than the California cousin, and the interior spaces were comparatively tight. Nature also caused differences. In Chicago, the front porch, almost a *sine qua non* in California, was replaced by an enclosed bay that fronted the living room and acted as a sunporch, which was usually furnished with pots of ferns and other greenery. The entrance was through a front door that led into a small entrance hall, much needed in the Midwest in order to screen out the frigid elements. But, as in the California bungalow, you then typically moved into a living room behind which were a dining room and kitchen on one side and the bathroom and bedrooms on the other. Built-in features were everywhere. And, as in California, the kitchen was usually painted white and filled with the latest gadgets.

A "bungalow belt," as the Chicagoans put it, surrounds the central city. It has been recognized by Chicagoans and, led by Mayor Richard Daly, they have focused awareness of it by instituting ordinances that protect many neighborhoods from intrusions of condominiums and encourage residents to take pride in place. The results are heartwarming.

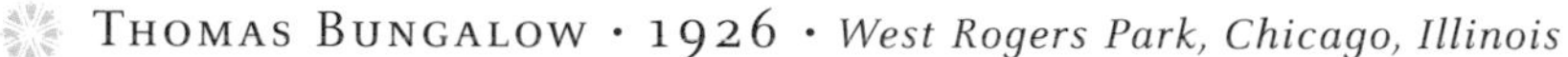

Thomas Bungalow · 1926 · *West Rogers Park, Chicago, Illinois*

Thomas Bungalow: the living room, the study

THOMAS BUNGALOW

Thomas Bungalow:
a cozy corner,
the dining room

MENUS & PROGRAMMES
ILLUSTRÉS

SIX

MODERNISM

Until the 1950s, the Midwest was not known for its heavy involvement with International Style architecture. In the 1920s, Europe was where the great iconoclasts—Walter Gropius, Ludwig Mies van der Rohe, and Le Corbusier—created their monuments to modernism. Stirrings of the new spirit could be detected on the East and West Coasts of the United States, but it was the advent of Nazi reaction in the 1930s that drove both Gropius and Mies to America—Gropius to Harvard and Mies to the Illinois Institute of Technology—where, through their teaching and their buildings, they gained hundreds of young recruits. Eventually the International Style took over almost all of the architectural schools where the litany of functionalism and abstraction dominated the curriculum and determined building style for almost a generation.

In the Midwest, Mies was naturally the greatest influence. Even Frank Lloyd Wright, a true Midwesterner, had to measure up to him. Although Wright promoted himself as a progressive, he was a Victorian conservative at heart. The Usonian houses that he produced after 1937 were intended to preserve the sanctity of the home and family. They were adorned with color in rich profusion, austerity be damned. Wright denounced the modernist creed whenever he got a chance. Significantly, he raised the question, "What is modernism?" a question that we have not yet answered.

Mies's architectural practice was mainly in public buildings; Wright's was mainly housing. Ironically, Mies's masterpiece was the Farnsworth House (1949–51) near Chicago. But as many critics, including the original owner, have pointed out, it is unlivable. In spite of the enormous popularity of his style, the Midwest remained basically conservative. At least in domestic architecture, the Midwesterners preferred their period revivals or, if they caught the new spirit, the soft modernism of what they called modernistic houses and what we call Streamline Moderne.

CENTURY-OF-PROGRESS EXPOSITION • 1933–1934

In 1933, the country was in the deepest throes of the Great Depression, and many people struggled with the problem of calling a world's fair "A Century-of-Progress Exposition." Thirteen million Americans were unemployed. Yet more than 22 million attended the fair in the two years of its existence. Obviously, it was successful in its supporters' aim not only to celebrate the great economic growth that had occurred in the nineteenth and early twentieth century but also to suggest that the setback of the Depression was only temporary and that much new growth was in store for the future.

If the aim of the fair's organizers was to raise the spirits of its visitors, the architectural setting certainly came up to their high expectations. The whole fair was laid out in architecture that expressed modernity, but the colors and shapes were fanciful in the extreme. It is significant that in the display of what the future might hold, the fair's architects did not go to the Bauhaus for ideas but went to what has been called "the architecture of entertainment." It was nothing that would put people off by its smack-

"House of Tomorrow" • 1934 • *Beverly Shores, Michigan*
George Fred Keck, architect

Armco-Ferrow House • 1934 • *Beverly Shores, Michigan*
Robert Smith Jr., architect • 2006 photo

Florida House • 1934 • *Beverly Shores, Michigan* • *Robert Law Weed, architect*

ing of intellectual depth as in the European school—no "theory" architecture, just some detail that would excite the senses but not too much.

It was in this spirit that the Home and Industrial Arts Group asked George Fred Keck to design a "House of Tomorrow," which was not really a model for future housing but a demonstration of what could be done with modern materials such as steel, glass, chrome plate, and plastic, whatever could be imagined for a new world. The three floors of the house were cantilevered from a central column, a form of construction probably taken from Frank Lloyd Wright's idea of floors hung from reinforced concrete piers. As with Wright, the reason for doing this had no real basis in need except that of pleasure. The same whimsy inspired Keck to devote the ground floor to an airplane hangar and a one-car garage.

The group's other houses, some by well-known architects, were more conventional in design but equally strong in the use of modern materials. In 1935, a number of these (some illustrated here) were brought in barges from the site of the fair to Beverly Shores not only as mementos but also as attractions to development. Unfortunately, they fell into various states of disrepair, but at present, there seems to be interest in reviving them perhaps as a museum of an idea that gave hope to the American people in troubled times.

· Home and Industrial Arts Group · Chicago, Illinois ·

Houses moved from the Century-in-Progress Exposition to Beverly Shores, Michigan, in 1935

"House of Tomorrow" · 1934 · *George Fred Keck (Chicago), architect*

Armco-Ferro House · 1934 · *Robert Smith Jr. (Ohio), architect*

Rostone House · 1934 · *Walter Scholer (Indiana), architect*

Florida House · 1934 · *Robert Law Weed (Miami, Florida), architect*

(Weed was one of the first Southern Modernists)

Jacobs House · 1937 · *Madison, Wisconsin*
Frank Lloyd Wright, architect

Photo by and courtesy of Pamela D. Kingsbury

USONIAN

Just before World War II, Frank Lloyd Wright had begun a new line of houses. With patriotic zeal he called them Usonians (a play on USA). They were his attempt (failed from the start) to develop a house with all the comforts of his Prairie-style dwellings but within the budgets of people with modest means. The first that was actually built, the Jacobs House (1936), was designed for a University of Wisconsin professor and his wife, and it was L-shaped with the kitchen and bedrooms in the long wing. This plan with variations was used again and again into the 1950s when the Christian house was designed and built. When the Christians asked Wright to design a house for them, they were young and only modestly funded, John being a science teacher at Purdue University. Like many of Wright's youthful clients, they expected him to be arrogant, but he was the opposite. He promised to give them a Usonian house that was based on his principles but less expensive than his Prairie-style buildings. And he did. During the five years that it took him to do the design, the Christians must have come upon a fortune, for Wright even designed the furniture, of which there is a lot. He gave specific instructions on where each piece was to be placed.

It is all there where he directed it to be, including a rug that displays Wright's abstract leitmotif for the house—the winged seed of the pinecone that is called "samara." Wright's organicism was in this case literal, but it also had a symbolic meaning since this work of nature was, according to theory, put together with every part related to the other parts and to the whole—the organic principle that Wright espoused. So a house should be, and Samara is.

One quickly notes its relation to the earlier Prairie-style houses. As in many of them, the entryway steps down into the living room, a movement that enhances an appreciation of Wright's manipulation of space. The fireplace is the focus of the room. The generous fenestration weds the outdoors to the indoors. But Samara has much more glass without art-glass designs to mar the view. It is bathed in light and is much more colorful than its Prairie cousin.

John and Catherine Christian House, "samara" · 1956

West Lafayette, Indiana · Frank Lloyd Wright, architect

CHRISTIAN HOUSE, "SAMARA"

Christian House "Samara": the living room, the dining room

CHRISTIAN HOUSE, "SAMARA"

Rush Creek Village • 1954–present • *Worthington, Ohio*

Theodore Van Fossen, architect

The story goes that Martha Wakefield, an Ohioan who was an admirer of Frank Lloyd Wright's Usonians, was visiting Taliesin in the 1950s. As she was saying goodbye, Wright is supposed to have said, "Go home, buy a Jeep and build a house for yourself. Then build a house for your next-door neighbor." And she did just that. She and her husband, Richard, discovered a designer, Theodore Van Fossen, who had worked as a carpenter and furniture maker for Wright, and the three of them found a large piece of rolling countryside in Worthington, a suburb of Columbus, Ohio. In 1954, they began building houses very much in the Wrightean vein. There are now forty-nine of them.

Each of these was set on roughly an acre of land—the relation to Wright's Broadacre City is obvious. Most of them were, moreover, around 2,000 square feet in floor plan, about the size of Wright's Usonian houses. Most of them are one story and plotted on an L-shaped floor plan. Again Wright's ideas were incorporated. All forty-nine of the homes were designed by Van Fossen. His designs surely reflected those of The Master, for he takes organizational principles and even details not only from the Usonian houses but also from other works of Wright's post-1940 period. Moreover, he relates them to each other with compatible forms carried from one house to another.

Smith Farm • 1948 • *Near Columbus, Ohio* • *Tony Smith, architect*

Tony Smith, who is best known for his painting and sculpture, worked in Frank Lloyd Wright's office in the late 1930s, just as Wright was developing his ideas for Usonian houses. After leaving Wright, he set up an architectural office in New York City and designed more than two dozen houses for friends. This is one of them.

Smith Farm: the living room, the backyard

SMITH FARM

EXPRESSIONISM

Sam and Ruth Ford House • 1947–50 • *Aurora, Illinois*

Bruce Goff, architect

In his early years, Bruce Goff described himself as "architect and composer." Sidney Robinson, who happens to be the present owner of Goff's Ford House, finds this coupling important in understanding Goff's complex work. Goff was a radical libertine in his architecture, a devoted modernist who wished to throw off formal restraints. He used found materials such as chunks of coal, gobs of glass, and even turkey inseminators because they pleased him. He despised precedent.

It was natural that he would admire the music of Claude Debussy, whose principal wish for his work was that it would express freedom. In 1961, Goff wrote, "We must understand Form and rhythm as part and parcel of idea and not a straight jacket ready-made into which ideas are poured. Debussy's understanding of this is helpful. He never had preconceived forms or structures before he had musical inspirations which he could discipline into their own forms and rhythms."

FORD HOUSE

Ford House:
the fireplace,
the main room

Modern Architecture

FORD HOUSE:
the main room,
the backyard

Goff the composer expressed his ideas on the player piano. Conveniently, he had never learned to play the piano. Instead, he punched holes in piano rolls in a pattern dictated simply by his imagination. The listeners then watched the perforations as Goff pumped the piano's pedals turning the rolls. What resulted was an unpremeditated cacophony. There is no question that Goff intended to shock his listeners, as he showed in the titles of his short pieces. One he called "Three Exaggerations: 1. going, 2. going, 3. gone!" Another was "Pabulum Pachydermatous." It is no wonder that, next to Debussy, he admired the music of Edgar Varèse and Harry Partch, who were contemporary iconoclasts.

In architecture, he admired the work of Frank Lloyd Wright because in it he saw the idea and the form wedded. But Goff was too much for Wright, who thought Goff made a mess of a great theory. Wright's buildings hug the ground. Goff's float. In fact, sometimes he suspends rooms from the ceiling and the floor moves under you, rendering the uneasy feeling experienced when crossing a bridge suspended from wires or ropes.

The Ruth Ford House is in a sense biographical. Its shape was inspired by Goff's familiarity as a navy veteran of World War II with Quonset hut ribs, which he adapted to frame the curved roofs of the house. He salvaged Plexiglas domes from military aircraft and turned them into skylights. He capitalized on the surprise attack.

Needless to say, all this is the exact opposite of Mies's Farnsworth House, which is just a few miles away.

EDITH FARNSWORTH HOUSE · 1949–50 · *Plano, Illinois*

Ludwig Mies van der Rohe, architect

In a sense, this house should not be in a book on homes. True, it was built for a person, Edith Farnsworth, a successful Chicago doctor who wanted a retreat from the city, but she rarely visited it once it was built. Although she understood its significance in the history of architecture, she was happy to sell it in 1962 to an Englishman, Peter Palumbo, who also made little use of it. It was a masterpiece of domestic architecture but one without a family. It is now a museum administered by the National Trust.

When Farnsworth decided to build, she wrote to the Museum of Modern Art and asked for the names of important architects. She was told that Le Corbusier, Frank Lloyd Wright, and Ludwig Mies van der Rohe were the best. Probably she chose Mies because he was nearby at the Illinois Institute of Technology in Chicago.

Usually Mies is associated with large public and commercial buildings, many of them skyscrapers; but as a young man in his native Germany, he had designed several houses, most of them for the Berlin bourgeoisie and in conventional architecture that we would call period revival styles. But just after serving in World War I, he began to draw significantly different buildings in glass and steel that, from the point of view of his contemporaries, appeared radical because they were without decorative devices. He eliminated ornamentation from his vocabulary and let his buildings speak from the qualities of their materials, some of them rich. He was identified as a modernist.

Urbig House • 1914
Potsdam-Neubabelsberg, Germany
Ludwig Mies van der Rohe, architect

Few of these projects were ever built, but he was able to advertise his modernity when he was appointed artistic director of the Weissenhofsiedlung, a housing colony erected near Stuttgart in order to show examples of the New Architecture. His German Pavilion at the International Exhibition in Barcelona in 1929 further promoted his career as a modernist, and he was appointed director of the Bauhaus the next year. He immigrated to the United States in 1938 and became director of the architectural school at the Illinois Institute of Technology, for which he began designing buildings.

Farnsworth House: the living room

The house that he created for Edith Farnsworth was probably the finest work of his life. He designed a one-story rectangular box in glass and steel. It is supported by eight wide-flange columns that carry the floor slab five feet above the ground in order to save it from floods of the Fox River. (They didn't!) The structure literally floats above the earth while taking in the natural landscape around it. The interior consists of one room in which a large wooden panel is placed so that it separates the living room from the bathroom, kitchen, and single bedroom.

FARNSWORTH HOUSE

When the house was published, the criticism was generally positive. It was recognized as a monument to Mies's "less is more" doctrine. It was a classic in abstraction, its static spaces contrasting strongly with Frank Lloyd Wright's flowing spaces. Then there were second thoughts. It was not a house; it was a temple to be admired rather than lived in. As Mies's biographer Franz Schulze put it, "certainly the house is more nearly a temple than a dwelling and it rewards aesthetic contemplation before it fulfills domestic necessity."

Probably Ludwig Mies van der Rohe was the most influential architect of the twentieth century. He created a style that was easily employed by hundreds of architects. Yet the Farnsworth House also marks a turning point in his influence. For some people, the absence of ornament, the abstraction, the function-be-damned attitude that the Farnsworth House projected seemed absurd. The result was the so-called "Post Modernism" in its many manifestations, some of them as absurd as Mies's purism. To his "less is more" doctrine, Robert Venturi retorted, "less is a bore."

Farnsworth House: the bedroom and kitchen

James Morrow House • 1949 • *Beverly Shores, Michigan*
Otto Kolb, architect

This house is tucked away on a mound overlooking Lake Michigan. It is a boxy International Style dwelling designed by Otto Kolb, a Swiss architect who received high praise when images of the house were published in Europe. Not a shocker like Mies's Farnsworth House, it nevertheless loves geometry. This has been softened by the present owner, who painted the garage door orange to give some life to the place. We should remind ourselves that not all International Style houses were white and black. Especially in the early examples, color was used. After all, at the Bauhaus the instructors taught painting. And Le Corbusier, being a painter as well as an architect, loved color.

The house is on the National Register of Historic Places.

MORROW HOUSE

Morrow House:
the main entrance,
the lakeside view,
the living room

Lustron House • 1947–50 • *Chesterton, Indiana*

After the almost complete shutdown of new house building during World War II, the nation suffered a serious postwar housing shortage. When construction materials became available, there naturally were attempts to rectify this situation. Levittown was one answer. Everywhere, but particularly in California, developers built tract housing and covered hundreds of acres of land with small houses in many styles. They paid no attention to ecology. They had a uniformity of plan well described in William H. Whyte's *Organization Man* (1956).

One of the responses to the shortage of housing was to stimulate the interest in prefabrication. It was not a new idea. Three identical prefabricated Gothic Revival houses were shipped around the Horn and constructed in California before the Civil War. In the late nineteenth and early twentieth centuries, Sears Roebuck and a number of "ready-cut" manufactured houses, including many bungalows, were sold throughout the country.

Lustron House: the utility room, the front yard

Zippy, created by and courtesy of Bill Griffith

LUSTRON HOUSE

The novelty of the Lustron House was that it was made with porcelain-enameled steel panels fastened to a steel frame. There had been experiments along this line in the 1930s, but they were never fully developed, due largely to the Great Depression. But in the mid-1940s housing crisis, these ideas were actually funded with federal grants. The Veterans Emergency Housing Act of 1946 even provided for the granting of surplus war-related factories to the new prefabrication industry. Congress promised government grants through the Reconstruction Finance Corporation.

LUSTRON HOUSE: the dining room, the bedroom vanity

Only two firms were chosen to produce steel houses: 1) the General Panel Corporation, interestingly representing the Bauhaus design partners Walter Gropius and Konrad Wachsman; and 2) Lustron, headed by Carl Strandlund, who had had experience making prefabricated steel buildings for White Castle restaurants and Standard Oil gas stations. Strandlund believed that his steel house was what "America had been waiting for." His enthusiasm moved the Reconstruction Finance Corporation to endorse his projects and to give him a loan of $15.5 million and the almost new but recently vacated Curtis-Wright aircraft plant in Columbus, Ohio. This was a tremendous boost since Columbus was a city with excellent air and railroad connections.

A number of delays occurred in starting production, but finally the first house was manufactured in November 1948. It was called the "Esquire" and it came in four colors—dove gray, desert tan, surf blue, and maize yellow. Its dimensions were 1,093 square feet with a range of built-ins. Heating came from panels in the ceiling from which the air was forced down into the rooms. The Esquire had only two bedrooms; later models, the Westchester and Newport, had three. Buyers sometimes complained about the metal shell collecting heat in the summer, but in general, most of them were happy about their purchases.

After receiving unprecedented loans and guarantees from the federal government, it seemed that Lustron would be a sure success. But even before production began in 1948, there were signs of trouble. For one thing, the Federal Housing Administration, which stood behind loans, warned lenders against extending credit to any construction company that engaged in modernist architecture. There was concern that the public was not ready for the International Style and that that apprehension would affect resale value. It is possible that the Lustron dealers who had to purchase the house materials before they left the factory were affected by the gloom spread by a government agency, as the potential buyers also might have been for they had to pay for the land on which their house would stand and for the labor costs and mortgage.

Nevertheless, the real problem besides the nervous government was the poor management of the Lustron Corporation. Since the idea of putting up steel houses was relatively new, it was natural that there would be areas of production where inefficiencies would occur. For example, the steel plates on the exterior of the houses were of a different size than those on the interior, making for awkwardness and, thus, expense. Distribution problems also arose. By the time these problems had been thought over and resolved, the housing crisis had passed. What Lustron needed was someone like Henry Kaiser, who had organized a shipbuilding industry almost overnight during World War II. Carl Strandlund, the CEO of the company, was enthusiastic and persistent but hardly a genius.

Government money was cut off in 1950 and the company closed its doors. Its failure proved to many people that the factory-made house was a disaster. But many of the almost 3,000 Lustron houses still exist in the Midwest (few are found on either the East or West Coasts) as a reminder of a period in American history when for a short time the government really cared about people with small incomes and wanted to preserve the tradition of the single-family home.

Harris House:
the southern front view,
the main entrance (pp. 150–51)

IRVING AND JOAN HARRIS HOUSE · 1996–98 · *Sawyer, Michigan*

Margaret McCurry, architect

Although Sawyer is on Lake Michigan, this house is several miles inland in farm country. The estate, landscaped by Maria Smithburg, is on the Galien River, and inlets from it provide the water element that is important to the mood of the house, which hovers on high ground over the river valley below.

The house looks like a farmhouse that has been enlarged to include several barns and sheds—"well-connected," as New Englanders might say. It is a series of abstractions of vernacular images very

HARRIS HOUSE

Harris House

appropriate to the rural site. It is pure Midwest, although it might also be pure New England if there were a few more hills in this part of Michigan.

The architect, Margaret McCurry, is a birthright Midwesterner who went to Vassar and then married Stanley Tigerman, the well-known Chicago architect. Although trained in interior design, she moved into architectural work after studying as a Loeb Fellow at the Harvard Graduate School of Design and then spending eleven years in the Chicago office of Skidmore, Owings and Merrill.

Though she is in partnership with her husband, she worked independently in this case and designed the house with the special needs of the Harris family in mind. It was built after the Harrises' sons were on their own. As their families began to enlarge, the Harrises realized that they must have a house that would serve many people. Because it is strung out on a long ridge, it looks large; however, as in the houses of most wealthy Americans, it is not overwhelming, certainly by European standards. Nevertheless, it can accommodate a good many people during their visits. All of the rooms on the first and second floors are well designed and spacious with high ceilings and white wall surfaces, but the living room is spectacular. It is a great hall rising two stories to a cathedral ceiling and is flooded with light, thanks in part to clerestory windows. Based on a symmetrical layout and closed at both the east and west ends with vertical panels that house the large fireplace and encase a narrow staircase, this disciplined room must teach the children good manners. At the same time, it is warm if not cozy. And as the family gathers around the fireplace, there is always music, a passion for the Harrises.

Harris House:
the hallway,
the living room,
the master bedroom

BIBLIOGRAPHICAL NOTE

Since we have visited all of the houses included in this book, I have used that fact as an excuse for putting many of my observations (and opinions) in it. But it also rests on a great many ideas presented by other people who have done more research than I have into the history of individual buildings. Frankly, I have accepted a great deal of material that is available in handouts at house museums. They cannot always be trusted, but my feeling is that they are, over the years, becoming more accurate, more critical, and certainly better written than they were fifteen to twenty years ago.

The amazing Google, though often off the mark, is a help in getting a head start on a subject. Most fascinating are the WPA guides to every state (and a number of cities) in the Union. God bless the editors of these relics of a bygone age for having given work to so many perceptive people and allowed them to roam in hitherto relatively untouched areas such as American domestic architecture. The WPA guides are old—all date from the late 1930s or early 1940s—but that is part of their charm and their usefulness, for they speak for an era unlike ours and, by the way, make us critical of the peculiarity of some of our own strongly held judgments.

There is no book on the history of Midwest architecture. The title of Wayne Andrews' *Architecture in Chicago and Mid-America* (1968) promises much, but it is mainly an album of beautiful pictures taken by the author. In the introduction to our book, I have already paid my compliments to another old volume, Dorothy and Richard Pratt's *The Guide to Early American Homes, North and South* (1956), which was my guide when I was living in the East. It is old, but it is pioneering at its best.

In the 1990s, the Society of Architectural Historians took on a project of trying through guides to the architecture of each state to do for our country what Nikolaus Pevsner did for England. Its task was ambitiously conceived but has slowed down for lack of money. It did produce two volumes on the Midwest: 1) David Gebhard and Gerald Mansheim's work on Iowa, and 2) Kathryn Bishop Eckert's book on Michigan, both published in 1993. Earlier, Frederick Koeper independently produced *Illinois Architecture* (1968), and much more recently, Ray E. Boomhower did the same for Indiana in his *Destination Indiana: Travels through Hoosier History* (2000). Following this, Bill Shaw produced a handsome volume on the architecture of the same state, *Historic Homes of Indiana* (2002). It has been a major source for items in our book. Guides to architecture in the cities and even small towns are appearing everywhere.

I have tried to give credit in the text to the books and articles that have been especially useful to me. There are, of course, many studies on individual architects. They are too numerous to list in a book of this size. The most writing has been done on Midwestern genius Frank Lloyd Wright. We have barely touched on his work. Enough is enough.

INDEX

A
Abele, Mary Pat, 60
Adam, James, 17
Adam, Robert, 17
Adam and Eve, 97
Adamesque. *See* Classical Revival
Age of Change, 33–36
  French Second Empire (Mansard), 53–63
  Gothic Revival, 36–44
  Italianate, 45–53
  Queen Anne, 64–71
  Richardsonian, 73–77
Age of Reform:
  Beaux-Arts, 84–89
  Chicago bungalow, 108–13
  Prairie style, 90–99
  Shingle style, 79–83
  Tudor Revival, 101–7
Agriculture, 89
Allen, Benjamin F., 53–57
Allen House, Wichita, Kansas, ix
"American Gothic" House, 40–41
Antiquities of Athens, The, 18, 29
Arbor Day, 89
"Arbor Lodge," 89
Architecture of Country Houses, 35
Armco-Ferrow House, 116, 117
Art Deco, ix
Art Center, De Moines, Iowa, ix
Arts and Crafts, 4, 36, 40, 68, 75, 107
Ashbee, Charles Robert, 36
Ashbee, Janet, 36–38
Asian influence, 79–83
Asymmetry, 34–36
Avery House, Alfred, 29–30

B
Barnett, George Ingham, 58
Baroque. *See* Georgian style
Bathrooms, 60
Bauhaus, 116, 141, 147
Beauties of Modern Architecture, The, 22
Beaux-Arts, ix, 75, 84–89
Bedrooms, 93
Beecher, Henry Ward, 53
Benjamin, Asher, 29
Beverly Shores, Michigan, 116–17
Bird, George Washington, 73–75
Bonaparte, Napoleon, 34
Bond, Carlyn, 60
Boone, Daniel, 13
Boone House, Nathan, 12–14
Boyington, William W., 53–57
Brick, 108
Broadacre City, 123
Brooks, Harold C., 50
Brown, B. Gratz, 58
Brown, John, 89
Buchanan, James, 89
Builder's Guide, The, 29
Bulfinch, Charles, 22
"Bungalow belt," 108
Byrne, Barry, 94–99

C
Cahokia, Illinois, 1–3
California bungalows, 108
Canals, xii–xiii
Carnahan, Jean, 58
Carnegie, Andrew, 68
Century-of-Progress Exposition, 116–17
Ceramics, American, 64
Change, Age of, 33–36
Chicago bungalow, 108–13
Chicago Water Tower and Pumping Station, 56
Christian House, John and Catherine, 117–21
Churches, Classical Revival and, 33–34
Clarke House, Henry B., 31
Classical Revival, 17–32, 33
  Small Town: Madison, Indiana, 18–28
  Elsewhere, 29–31
Cleveland, Grover, 89
Closets, 60
Cobb, Henry Ives, 76–77
Cologne, Germany, 33
Composite order, 26

Conn House, C. G., 84–87
Conservative, The, 89
Conspicuous consumption, 64
Corduroy roads, xiii
Corinthian order/colonnade, 33, 84
Cornet, significance of, 84, 87
Costigan, Francis:
  Captain Charles Lewis Shrewsbury House, 24–25
  House, 26–28
  James Lanier Mansion, 22–23
Curtis-Devin House, 34
Curtis-Wright aircraft plant, 147

D
Daly, Richard, 108
Darrow, Clarence, 102
Davis, A.J., xiv
Debussy, Claude, 128, 133
Dewing, Thomas, 83
Downing, Andrew Jackson, 34–36
Dunn Cabin, 5
Dvorák, Antonín, xiv

E
Early Architecture of Madison, Indiana, The, 28
Eastlake, Charles Locke, 64–65, 68
École des Beaux-Arts, Paris, 36
Elmslie, George Grant, ix, 97
Emigrants, European, xiv
Emporia Gazette, 101
European emigrants, xiv
Evans House, John L. and Florence N., 103–7
Expressionism, 128–33
Eyre, Wilson, 75, 79–83

F
Faragher, John Mack, 13
Farnsworth House, Edith, xiv, 115, 133, 134–40, 141
Federal Housing Administration, 148
Federal style. *See* Classical Revival
First Presbyterian Church of Kinsman, Ohio, 35
Florida House, 116, 117
Ford House, Sam and Ruth, vii, 128–33
Foster and Liebe, 75
Foursquare House, 100
Fowler, Orson Squire, 53
Franke House, John B. and Amelia, 94–99
Freer House, Charles Lang, 75, 78–83
French influence, 1–3, 17
French Second Empire style, 36, 53–63

G
Gaff, James and John, 46
Gaff Mansion, Thomas, 45–49
Galloway Cabin, 6–7
Gardens, "Hillforest," endpages, 48, 49
General Panel Corporation, 147
Georgian style, 12–13, 17
"Gingerbread," 68
Glessner Mansion, John G., 76
Godberson, Byron, ix
Goethe, Wolfgang, 33
Goff, Bruce, 128–33
Goodhue, Bertram, ix
Gospel of Wealth, 68
Gothic architecture, ix
Gothic Revival, 33–44, 56
Gothic Revival House(s), 44, 144
Grace, F. A., 50
Grant House, General Ulysses S., 35
Great Depression, 116–17, 146
Greece, expressions of, 33
Greene, Charles and Henry, 92, 93
Greenleaf, Carl D. and Deacon, 87
Greeley, Horace, 58
Griffin, Walter Burley, 97
Griffith, Bill, 144
Gropius, Walter, 115, 147
Guide to Early American Homes, North and South, The, x

H
Hackley House, Charles, i, 65–71
Harris Hous, Irving and Joan, 149–53
"Heartland Tour," ix
Herculaneum, 17
"Hillforest," endpages, xiv, 45–49
"Hillside Cottage," 72–75
Hints on Household Taste, 64, 68
Home and Industrial Arts Group, 117
"Homestead, The," 4
Homestead Act, 89
"Honolulu House," 50–51

Hopkins, David S., 65–71
Horizontality, 90–92
"House of Tomorrow," 116, 117
Hubbard, Elbert, 36–40
Hubbell, Frederick M., 56
Hull, Cordell, 4
Hume, Thomas, 68
Hunt, Richard Morris, 36
Hunter House, Dard, 5, 36–40
Hutslar, Donald A., 4

I
Iannelli, Alfonso, 97
If the Walls Could Talk:
  The Story of Missouri's First Families, 58
Immigration, immigrants, xii, xiv
Interior design, 64–65
International Studio, 38
International Style, 115, 134–48
Iolani Palace, Honolulu, 50
Iowa Governor's Mansion, 32–33, 53–57
Italianate, xiv, 34–36, 45–53
Italian Villa style. *See* Italianate

J
Jackson, Andrew, 4
Jacobs House, 117
Japanese art and influence, 64, 79–83, 108
Jefferson, Thomas, 40
Joslyn Art Museum, Omaha, Nebraska, ix

K
Kaiser, Henry, 148
Keck, George Fred, 116, 117
Kelly Brothers Manufacturing Company of Muskegon, 68
Kingsbury, Pamela, ix
Kolb, Otto, 141–43

L
Lafever, Minard, 22, 29
Lakes, xii–xiii
Lanier Mansion, James, 22–23
Latrobe, Benjamin Henry, 22, 33–34
Lautz, William Henry, 103–7
Le Corbusier, 115, 135, 141
Le Poincet House, xiv, xv, 1–3
Levittown, 144
Leyland, Frederick R., 79
Lincoln Cabin, Abraham, 8–9
"Litchfield," xiv, 35
Living rooms, 93
Log Architecture of Ohio, The, 4
Log Cabin:
  French Interpretation, 1–3
  Yankee Log Cabin, 4–11
Louisiana Purchase Exposition, 2
Louvre, 36
Lustron House, 144–48

M
Macadam, xiii
Madison, Indiana, 18–28
Mahoney, Marion, 97
Mansard-roof style, 36, 53–63
Mansart, Francois, 36
"Mansion House, The," 31
Master, The. *See* Wright, Frank Lloyd
Maybeck, Bernard, 92, 93
McCurry, Margaret, 149–53
Meganhoffen, Louis, 36
Meier, Richard, ix
Michigan Road, 18
Midwest:
  boundaries and geography of, xi
  settlement of, xi–xiv
  culture of, xiv
Mies van der Rohe, Ludwig, xiv, 115, 133, 134–40, 141
Mission Inn, Riverside, California, 38
Mission Revival, 87
Missouri Governor's Mansion, 58–63
Modern Builder's Guide, The, 29
Modernism, 114–53
  Century-of-Progress Exposition, 116–17
  Expressionism, 128–33
  International Style, 134–48
  Modern Vernacular, 149–53
  Usonian, 117–27
"Monkey Trial," 102
Monticello, 40
Morgan, Benjamin, 29–30
Morris, William, 36, 38, 107
Morrow House, James, 141–43

Morton House, J. Sterling and Carolyn Joy, 88–89
"Mountain House," v, 36–40
Mountain House Press, 40
Mouthpiece, 84–87
Muskegon, Michigan, 65–72

N
Napoleon, 34
Napoleon III, 36
Nationalism, xiv
National Road, xiii
Nebraska City News, 89
Nebraska State Capitol, ix
Neff Cottage, 42
Neo-Gothic, 76

O
Octagon House, 52–53
Octagon House, The: A Home for All, 53
Organ and recordings, 97
Organization Man, 144
Osbourne House, Isle of Wight, 60
Owen, David Dale, 43
Owen Laboratory, 43

P
Palladio, Andrea, 17
Palmer, Potter, 76
Palumbo, Peter, 135
Partch, Harry, 133
Peabody and Stearns, 76
"Peacock Room," 79
Pei, I. M., ix
Perry, Admiral, 64
Pewabic Pottery, 64, 79, 83
Piano, 133
Pipe organ, 97
Pompeii, 17
Pope, Alexander, 49
Post-on-sill structure, 2
Prairie style, 34, 90–99, 102, 108, 118
Pratt House, Abner, 50–51
Pratt, Dorothy and Richard, x
Proudfoot House, William Thomas, 72–75
Proodfoot and Bird, 72–75
Proudfoot, Bird and Rawson, 75
Purcell, William Gray, 97

Q
Queen Anne style, 49, 64–71, 79, 102
Quonset huts, 133

R
Railroads, xiii
Reconstruction Finance Corporation, 146, 147
"Red Rocks," 101–2
Renwick, James, 43
Revett, Nicholas, 18, 29
Reynolds, John, 1–2
Richardson, H. H., 73, 76
Richardsonian, 73–77
Rivers, xii–xiii
Roads, xiii
Robbins Hunter Museum, 29–30
Robinson, Sidney, 128
Rogers, Isaiah, xiv, 49
Romanesque. *See* Richardsonian
Romanticism, 33
Rome, expressions of, 33
Rookwood, 64
Roosevelt, Franklin, 4
Roosevelt, Theodore, 102
Rostone House, 117
Route 40, xiii
Roycroft Arts and Crafts, 36, 38
Rubber mouthpiece, 84–87
Rush Creek Village, 114–15, 122–23

S
Saarinen, Eliel, ix
"Samara," 117–21
Sargeant Farm, 10–11
Sargent, John Singer, 83
Saucier House, 1–3
Scholer, Walter, 117
Schulze, Franz, 140
Scopes, John, 102
Scully, Vincent, Jr., 79
Shaw, Richard Norman, 64, 73
Sherman House, Watts, 73, 75
Shingle style, 68, 76, 79–83
Shrewsbury House, Captain Charles Lewis, 24–25

Skidmore, Owings and Merrill, 150
Small Town: Madision, Indiana, 18–28
Smith House, John E., 31
Smith Cabin, Joseph, 4
Smith House, Joseph, Jr., 31
Smith, Joseph, III, 4
Smith, Robert, Jr., 116, 117
Smith Farm, Tony, 124–27
Smithburg, Maria, 149
Society of Architectural Historians, ix
St. Paul's Episcopal Church, 34
Stowe, Harriet Beecher, 53
Stradlund, Carl, 147, 148
Streamline Moderne, 115
Strong, Samuel, 84–87
Stuart, James, 18, 29
Studebaker House, Clement, 76–77
Sullivan House, Jeremiah, ii, vi, 18–21
Sullivan, Louis, 107
Swiss Chalet, 108

T
T-Square Club, 75
Taliesin, 93, 102
Temple of the Winds, Athens, 22
"Terrace Hill," 32–33, 53–57
Thayer, Abbott, 83
Theseum, Athens, 29
Thomas Bungalow, 109–13
Tigerman, Stanley, 150
Tomek House, Ferdinand and Emily, 90–93, back jacket
Transportation, xii–xiii
Trees, 89
Trinity Church, Boston, 75
Tryon, Dwight, 83
Tudor Revival, 101–7
Turner, Frederick Jackson, 13

U
Uncle Tom's Cabin, 53
Underground Railroad, 89
Unity Temple, 97
Urbig House, 136
U. S. Capitol, Washington, D.C., 33
Usonian style, 117–27

V
Van Fossen, Theodore, 122–23
Varèse, Edgar, 133
Veblen, Thorstein, 64
Venturi, Robert, 140
Vernacular, Modern, 149–53
Vitruvius, 17

W
Wachman, Konrad, 147
Wakefield, Martha and Richard, 123
Washington, George, 34
Weed, Robert Law, 116, 117
Whistler, James McNeill, 79
White, Stanford, 79, 81
White House, William Allen and Sallie Lindsay, 101–2
Whyte, William H., 144
Wichita City Hall, 75
Wight & Wight, 101–2
Willatzen, Andrew, 97
Windle, Ann, 24
Windle, John T., 22, 28
Wofford, Ted, 60
Woodbury County Courthouse, Sioux City, Iowa, ix
Wood, Grant, xiv, 40–41
Woody, 4
World's Columbian Exhibition of 1893, 76, 84
Worthington Building, 15
WPA, WPA guides, x, 2
Wright, Frank Lloyd, ix, 22, 34, 123, 125, 135, 140
  Barry Byrne, influence on, 94
  Bruce Goff, influence on, 133
  Christian House, 117–21
  Jacobs House, 117
  Modernism and, 115
  Tomek House, 90–93, back jacket
  Usonian style and, 115, 117–27
  White House, 102
"Wynkook," 34

Y
Yankee migrants, xi

Z
Zippy, 144

ACKNOWLEDGMENTS

Many Midwesterners must be thanked for their contributions to this book. They include Mary Pat Abele, John E. Christian, Marcia Rees Conrad, Gail Ettinger, Becky Fitzgerald, Alan Grinsfelder, Christine Hampton, Joan Harris, Dard Hunter III, Pamela D. Kingsbury, Margery Ziesel Krumwiede, Judith McBrien, Marcia McCurry, Jean McDaniel, Jim Morrow, Don Prosser, Sidney Robinson, Pauline Saliga, John Staicer, Meg and Tim Shelly, C. W. Stewart, Ron and Marty Thomas, Irene Vertikoff, Ann Windle, and Tamara M. Zoller.

Organizations have also helped. Among them are the following: Hillforest Historical Foundation, Historic Madison, Inc., Historic New Harmony, Landmark Preservation Council of Illinois, Lindenwood University, Merrill-Palmer Institute, Muskegon Museum, and National Trust for Historic Preservation.

As always in our experience with Gibbs Smith, Publisher, we are indebted to managing editor Madge Baird and to the editorial staff—Lisa Anderson, Leticia Le Bleu, Sarah Rigley, and Renee Wald; to the production staff—Marty Lee and Natalie Wilde; and to indexer Rachel Lyon. Our special thanks go to Linda Nimori, who as editor has disciplined us and tidied up the manuscript. Kurt Hauser's graphics and talent for organization produced a beautiful book.